Core Learning Standards for Mathematics Grade 4

Operations and Algebraic Thinking (Mondays)	
Interpret a multiplication equation as a comparison.	p. 4 #1 p. 7 #1 p. 10 #1 p. 13 #1 p. 19 #1 p. 22 #1 p. 25 #1 p. 31 #4 p. 34 #1 p. 37 #1 p. 46 #4 p. 49 #4 p. 52 #1 p. 55 #1 p. 61 #1 p. 64 #3 p. 76 #2 p. 79 #2 p. 82 #1 p. 85 #1
Multiply or divide to solve word problems involving multiplicative comparison.	p. 1 #1 p. 13 #4 p. 22 #2 p. 40 #3 p. 43 #4 p. 52 #2 p. 58 #2 p. 61 #3 p. 67 #1 p. 76 #3
Solve multistep word problems posed with whole numbers. Represent these problems using equations with a letter standing for the unknown quantity.	p. 4 #3 p. 7 #3 p. 10 #1–2 p. 13 #3 p. 16 #2 p. 19 #4 p. 28 #3 p. 31 #1 p. 34 #3 p. 37 #3 p. 40 #3 p. 43 #4 p. 46 #1 p. 49 #2 p. 55 #2 p. 61 #3 p. 64 #1 p. 70 #1, 4 p. 73 #1 p. 76 #1, 3 p. 79 #1 p. 82 #3 p. 85 #2–3 p. 88 #3
Find all factor pairs for a whole number in the range 1–100. Determine whether a whole number is a multiple of a given number. Determine whether a whole number is prime or composite.	p. 1 #3 p. 7 #2 p. 10 #3 p. 19 #3 p. 28 #2 p. 31 #3 p. 37 #2 p. 40 #1 p. 49 #1 p. 52 #4 p. 58 #3 p. 61 #2 p. 64 #2 p. 67 #2 p. 70 #3 p. 73 #2 p. 82 #2 p. 88 #2
Generate a number or shape patterns that follows a given rule.	p. 1 #4 p. 4 #4 p. 7 #4 p. 10 #4 p. 13 #2 p. 16 #3–4 p. 19 #2 p. 22 #3–4 p. 25 #3–4 p. 28 #4 p. 31 #2 p. 34 #4 p. 37 #4 p. 40 #2, 4 p. 43 #3 p. 46 #2–3 p. 49 #3 p. 52 #3 p. 55 #3–4 p. 58 #4 p. 61 #4 p. 64 #4 p. 67 #3–4 p. 70 #2 p. 73 #3–4 p. 76 #4 p. 79 #3–4 p. 82 #4 p. 85 #4 p. 88 #4 Tuesdays p. 34 #2 p. 49 #3
Number and Operations in Base Ten (Tuesdays)	
Recognize that a digit in one place represents ten times what it represents in the place to its right.	p. 4 #1 p. 7 #1 p. 10 #1, 3 p. 16 #1 p. 22 #1 p. 28 #1 p. 31 #1 p. 37 #1 p. 46 #1 p. 49 #1 p. 55 #1 p. 58 #1 p. 61 #1 p. 64 #3 p. 73 #2
Read and write numbers using numerals, names, and expanded form. Compare numbers using >, =, and <.	p. 1 #1,3 p. 7 #3 p. 10 #2 p. 13 #1 p. 16 #2 p. 22 #2–3 p. 25 #2 p. 28 #3 p. 34 #1, 4 p. 40 #3 p. 43 #2 p. 46 #2 p. 52 #2–3 p. 55 #2 p. 64 #2 p. 70 #1–2 p. 76 #2–3 p. 79 #1–2 p. 85 #1–2 p. 88 #2
Use place value understanding to round numbers.	p. 1 #2 p. 7 #2 p. 13 #2 p. 19 #2 p. 25 #3 p. 28 #2 p. 31 #2 p. 37 #2 p. 40 #2 p. 43 #1 p. 49 #2 p. 52 #1 p. 58 #2 p. 61 #2 p. 67 #2 p. 73 #1 p. 76 #1 p. 82 #1 p. 88 #1
Add and subtract multi-digit numbers.	p. 1 #4 p. 4 #3 p. 7 #4 p. 10 #3 p. 13 #4 p. 16 #4 p. 19 #4 p. 31 #4 p. 34 #3 p. 37 #4 p. 40 #1 p. 46 #3 p. 55 #3 p. 58 #3 p. 61 #4 p. 64 #1 p. 67 #1 p. 73 #4 p. 82 #3 p. 85 #3
Multiply—using equations, arrays, and/or area models.	p. 4 #4 p. 16 #3 p. 19 #3 p. 34 #2 p. 40 #3 p. 43 #3–4 p. 49 #4 p. 52 #3 p. 61 #3 p. 67 #3 p. 70 #4 p. 73 #3 p. 79 #3 p. 82 #4 p. 88 #4
Find quotients and remainders—using equations, arrays, and/or area models.	p. 10 #4 p. 22 #4 p. 25 #4 p. 28 #4 p. 31 #3 p. 37 #3 p. 46 #4 p. 49 #3 p. 55 #4 p. 58 #4 p. 64 #4 p. 67 #4 p. 70 #3 p. 76 #4 p. 79 #4 p. 85 #4
Number and Operations—Fractions (Wednesdays)	
Explain why a fraction *a/b* is equivalent to a fraction *(n × a)/(n × b)*.	p. 2 #3 p. 5 #1 p. 8 #2 p. 11 #2 p. 14 #2 p. 20 #1 p. 23 #2 p. 26 #4 p. 29 #1 p. 32 #2 p. 35 #1–2 p. 38 #1–2 p. 41 #1 p. 44 #1–2 p. 47 #1 p. 50 #1–2 p. 53 #1 p. 56 #1 p. 59 #1 p. 68 #1 p. 74 #1
Compare two fractions with different numerators and different denominators using >, =, or <.	p. 2 #2 p. 5 #2 p. 11 #3 p. 17 #1–2 p. 20 #3 p. 23 #3 p. 26 #1–2 p. 29 #2 p. 32 #3 p. 35 #3 p. 41 #2 p. 62 #2 p. 83 #1
Understand a fraction as a sum of fractions; decompose fractions, add and subtract mixed numbers, and solve word problems by using visual fraction models.	p. 2 #4 p. 5 #4 p. 8 #3 p. 14 #4 p. 17 #4 p. 20 #2 p. 23 #4 p. 26 #4 p. 32 #4 p. 38 #3–4 p. 41 #3 p. 44 #3 p. 47 #2 p. 48 Brain Stretch p. 50 #3 p. 53 #2, 4 p. 54 Brain Stretch p. 56 #2–3 p. 59 #2 p. 65 #2 p. 68 #3 p. 69 Brain Stretch p. 71 #2–3 p. 74 #2 p. 77 #2 p. 80 #3 p. 83 #3 p. 86 #3–4 p. 89 #2–4

Visit www.creativeteaching.com to find out how this book correlates to Common Core and/c

Multiply a fraction by a whole number, and solve word problems by using visual fraction models.	p. 15 Brain Stretch　p. 17 #4　p. 29 #4　p. 41 #4　p. 44 #4　p. 47 #3–4 p. 50 #4　p. 53 #3　p. 59 #4　p. 62 #3–4　p. 65 #4　p. 68 #4　p. 71 #4　p. 74 #4 p. 77 #3–4　p. 80 #4　p. 83 #4　p. 89 #4　Friday　p. 48 #3
Express a fraction with denominator 10 as an equivalent fraction with denominator 100.	p. 11 #2　p. 23 #2　p. 29 #1　p. 32 #2, 4　p. 38 #3　p. 41 #3　p. 44 #3 p. 50 #1, 3　p. 59 #2　p. 71 #2
Use decimal notation for fractions $x/10$ or $x/100$.	p. 5 #3　p. 8 #4　p. 11 #4　p. 14 #3　p. 17 #3　p. 26 #3　p. 35 #4　p. 59 #3 p. 68 #2　p. 71 #1　p. 74 #3　p. 77 #1　p. 80 #1　p. 83 #2　p. 89 #1
Compare (using >, =, or <) two decimals to hundredths by reasoning about their size.	p. 11 #1　p. 14 #1　p. 20 #4　p. 29 #3　p. 56 #4　p. 65 #3　p. 80 #2　p. 86 #1

Measurement and Data (Thursdays & Fridays)

Know relative sizes of measurement units within one system of units. Record measurement equivalents in a two-column table.	Fridays　p. 3 #1, Brain Stretch　p. 9 #1–3, Brain Stretch　p. 12 #1–2　p. 18 #1–3 p. 21 #1–2　p. 24 #1, 2　p. 27 Brain Stretch　p. 30 #1–3　p. 33 #1–2　p. 39 #1–3 p. 42 Brain Stretch　p. 45 Brain Stretch　p. 51 #1–2　p. 57 #1–2　p. 60 #1–2 p. 63 Brain Stretch　p. 69 #1–2　p. 72 #1–2　p. 84 #1–3, Brain Stretch　p. 90 #1–2
Solve word problems involving measurement.	Fridays　p. 3 #2, 4, Brain Stretch　p. 6 #1–7　p. 9 #3, Brain Stretch　p. 12 #2–3, Brain Stretch　p. 15 #3, Brain Stretch　p. 18 #2–3, Brain Stretch　p. 21 #3, Brain Stretch　p. 24 #3　p. 27 #4–5, Brain Stretch　p. 30 #2–4, Brain Stretch p. 33 #2, 4, Brain Stretch　p. 36 #3–5, Brain Stretch　p. 39 #2–3, Brain Stretch p. 42 #3–5, Brain Stretch　p. 45 #1–5, Brain Stretch　p. 48 #2–3, Brain Stretch p. 51 #3, Brain Stretch　p. 54 #1–5, Brain Stretch　p. 57 #3, Brain Stretch p. 60 #3, Brain Stretch　p. 63 #1, 3, Brain Stretch　p. 66 #1–5 p. 69 #4, Brain Stretch　p. 72 #3–4, Brain Stretch　p. 75 #2–3, Brain Stretch p. 78 #2, 6, Brain Stretch　p. 81 #1–6　p. 84 #3–4, Brain Stretch　p. 87 #2–3 p. 90 #3–4　Tuesday　p. 67 #1
Apply the area and perimeter formulas for rectangles.	Fridays　p. 3 #3　p. 9 #4, Brain Stretch　p. 12 #4, Brain Stretch　p. 18 #4 p. 21 #4　p. 24 #4　p. 30 #4　p. 33 #3–4　p. 39 #4　p. 51 #4　p. 57 #4　p. 60 #4 p. 69 #3–4　p. 72 #4　p. 75 Brain Stretch　p. 84 #3　p. 90 #2, 4
Make a line plot to display a data set of measurements in fractions of a unit.	Fridays　p. 48 #1　p. 63 #2　p. 75 #1　p. 78 #1　p. 87 #1
Recognize angles as geometric shapes that are formed wherever two rays share a common endpoint.	Thursdays　p. 2 #4　p. 8 #3–4　p. 11 #3–4　p. 14 #2　p. 23 #2　p. 29 #2 p. 32 #4　p. 38 #2　p. 41 #1　p. 44 #2, 4　p. 47 #2–3　p. 50 #2　p. 53 #2 p. 59 #3　p. 62 #4　p. 65 #2　p. 74 #4　p. 80 #2–3　p. 86 #all　p. 89 #1
Measure and sketch angles in whole-number degrees.	Thursdays　p. 17 #2　p. 26 #2　p. 32 #1　p. 35 #2–3　p. 38 #1　p. 41 #1, 2 p. 47 #1　p. 50 #1, 4　p. 53 #1–2　p. 56 #2　p. 59 #1–2, 4　p. 62 #2　p. 68 #2 p. 71 #1　p. 89 #2
Recognize angle measure as additive.	Thursdays　p. 23 #3　p. 26 #3　p. 38 #2　p. 47 #2　p. 50 #4　p. 56 #3　p. 59 #2 p. 62 #4　p. 65 #3　p. 74 #3　p. 77 #4　p. 83 #3　p. 89 #4　Friday　p. 84 #5

Geometry (Thursdays)

Draw and identify points, lines, line segments, rays, angles, and perpendicular and parallel lines.	p. 2 #1–2　p. 5 #1–2　p. 8 #1, 3　p. 11 #1　p. 14 #1–2　p. 17 #1–2　p. 20 #1–2 p. 23 #1–2　p. 26 #1–2　p. 29 #1–2, 4　p. 32 #1–2　p. 35 #1–3　p. 38 #1 p. 39 #1　p. 41 #2–3　p. 44 #1　p. 47 #1, 3　p. 50 #1, 3　p. 53 #1–3 p. 56 #1–2, 4　p. 59 #1, 3–4　p. 62 #1–2　p. 65 #1–2, 4　p. 68 #1–2　p. 71 #1–2 p. 74 #1–2　p. 77 #1–2　p. 80 #1–3　p. 81 Brain Stretch　p. 83 #2 p. 87 Brain Stretch　p. 89 #1–2
Classify two-dimensional figures based on the presence or absence of parallel or perpendicular lines, or angles of a specified size.	p. 2 #2　p. 5 #2–4　p. 8 #2　p. 11 #1–2　p. 14 #4　p. 17 #3　p. 20 #3–4 p. 23 #4　p. 26 #2　p. 29 #3–4　p. 32 #1–2　p. 35 #2–4　p. 38 #1, 3–4 p. 41 #1–3　p. 44 #2, 4　p. 47 #1, 3–4　p. 50 #2–3　p. 53 #1–2　p. 56 #2–3 p. 59 #1　p. 62 #2–3　p. 65 #2　p. 68 #2–4　p. 71 #1, 3　p. 74 #3　p. 77 #2–3 p. 80 #2–3　p. 81 Brain Stretch　p. 83 #1–2　p. 86 #all　p. 87 Brain Stretch p. 89 #1–2
Recognize a line of symmetry.	p. 2 #3　p. 14 #3　p. 32 #3　p. 44 #3　p. 53 #4　p. 71 #4　p. 89 #3

Visit www.creativeteaching.com to find out how this book correlates to Common Core and/or State Standards.

Student Assessment

Customize page 93 to reflect the standards you are working on. Simply write the standard numbers in the columns across the top.

MONDAY — Operations and Algebraic Thinking

1 Which property of multiplication is shown?

$8 \times 5 = 40 \qquad 5 \times 8 = 40$

A. associative

B. commutative

C. identity

2 Circle the unknown quantity in the equation.

$17 + 2 + x = 22$

3 Label the numbers as prime (P) or composite (C).

A. 7 _____

B. 18 _____

C. 61 _____

4 Find the missing number in the sequence.

144, 133, 122, _____, 100

TUESDAY — Operations in Base Ten

1 Which digit is in the hundreds place?

900,500 _____

2 Round the number to the nearest ten.

137,878 _____

3 Compare using >, <, or =.

12,898 ☐ 12,839

4 20 + 50 = _____

WEDNESDAY — Fractions

1 Write the fraction that names the shaded part.

2 Which fraction is larger? Write < or >.

$$\frac{1}{4} \quad \square \quad \frac{1}{2}$$

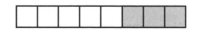

3 Complete the equivalent fraction.

$$\frac{1}{5} = \frac{\quad}{10}$$

4 Complete the addition statement.

$$\frac{3}{8} = \underline{\quad} + \underline{\quad}$$

THURSDAY — Geometry

1 Draw and label a point.

2 Classify the following pair of lines.

A. intersecting

B. parallel

C. perpendicular

3 How many lines of symmetry?

M _____

4 What fraction of a turn is this angle?

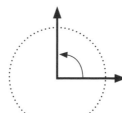

A. $\frac{1}{4}$ turn

B. $\frac{3}{4}$ turn

C. 1 full turn

D. $\frac{1}{2}$ turn

1 Complete the table.

Feet	Inches
1	12
2	
3	
4	

2 Liam walked 1.4 km to the beach. How many meters did he walk? Make a table for kilometers and meters to help you.

3 Shade in a shape with an area of 9 square units. What is the perimeter of your shape?

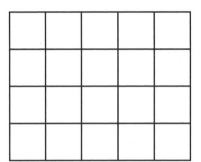

4 What time does Laura have to leave to be at home by 3:15 if the trip takes 90 minutes? Complete the number line to show your work.

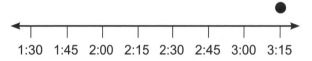

1:30   1:45   2:00   2:15   2:30   2:45   3:00   3:15

BRAIN STRETCH

Charlie and his friends want to see their favorite baseball team play this weekend. A ticket to the game costs $32.50.

a) How much will it cost for four people to attend the game?

b) If the game begins at 1:00 p.m. and it takes Charlie and his friends 1.5 hours to get to the field, when should they leave?

c) If a program costs $5.25, how much change will Charlie get if he pays with a $10 bill?

MONDAY — Operations and Algebraic Thinking

1 Which expression is equal to 4 × 5?

A. 5 + 5 + 5 + 5

B. 4 + 4 + 4 + 4

C. 5 × 5 + 4

2 Fill in the blank to make the equation true.

56 − _____ = 25 − 10

3 Kara bought a DVD for $22 and a CD for less than the cost of the DVD. Let c represent the cost of the CD. Write an inequality to show the cost of the CD.

c [   ] _____

4 Write the first 5 terms of this pattern:

Start at 10 and add 6 each time.

_____, _____, _____, _____, _____

TUESDAY — Operations in Base Ten

1 5 hundreds = _____ ones

2 What is the value of the underlined digit?

<u>2</u>34,761 _____

3 4,000 − 100 =

4 Draw a model to find the product.

7 × 7 =

WEDNESDAY — Fractions

1 Complete the equivalent fraction.

$$\frac{1}{4} = \frac{\quad}{12}$$

2 Which fraction is larger? Write < or >.

$$\frac{1}{6} \quad \boxed{\phantom{<}} \quad \frac{1}{10}$$

$\frac{1}{6}$					
$\frac{1}{10}$									

3 a) Represent $\frac{11}{100}$ on the place value model.

b) Write the fraction as a decimal.

Hundreds	Tens	Ones	.	Tenths	Hundredths
			.		

4 There are 12 markers in the box.
Half of the markers are red.
How many of the markers are **not** red?

THURSDAY — Geometry

1 Draw and label a ray.

2 Classify the following pair of lines.
Circle all the descriptions that apply.

A. intersecting

B. parallel

C. perpendicular

3 Describe the polygon.

Name _____

Number of obtuse angles _____

Number of acute angles _____

4 An obtuse triangle has

A. one 90˚ angle

B. one angle greater than 90˚

C. all angles less than 90˚

Ben conducted a survey of his cousins to see how many books they read in a month. He displayed the data as a pictograph.

Number of Books Read

Spencer	◆ ◆ ◆ ◆ ◆ ◆
Ben	◆ ◆ ◆ ◆ ◆ ◆ ◆ ◆
Madelyn	◆ ◆ ◆ ◆ ◆ ◆ ◆
Megan	◆ ◆ ◆ ◆ ◆
Michael	◆ ◆ ◆ ◆
Kaitlyn	◆ ◆ ◆ ◆ ◆ ◆ ◆ ◆ ◆

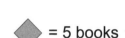 ◆ = 5 books

1 How many books were read altogether? _____

2 Who read the fewest books? _____

3 Which two people read the same number of books? _____

4 How many books did Michael and Ben read together? _____

5 How many more books did Kaitlyn read than Spencer? _____

6 How many fewer books did Michael read than Megan? _____

7 What is the range of the number of books read? _____

BRAIN STRETCH

Rick is older than Miguel. Miguel is older than Betty. Betty is older than Tina, and Vivienne is older than Rick. Who the oldest? Who is the youngest?

1 Write a multiplication expression for the statement.

4 times as many as ◆◆◆◆

2 Is the number 11 a prime number or a composite number? Build rectangles to show your answer. How many rectangles can you make?

3 Kas is 10 years older than Dina. Let y represent Dina's age in years. Write an equation to show Dina's age in years.

4 Create a repeating pattern by coloring.

OOOOOOOOO

1 4 thousands = _____ tens

2 Round 276 to the nearest hundred. Use a number line to help decide if 276 is closer to 200 or 300.

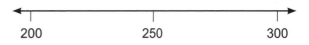

200   250   300

3 Compare using >, <, or =.

937,159 ☐ 997,122

4 600 + 3,000 =

1 Write the fraction that names the shaded part.

2 Complete the equivalent fractions.

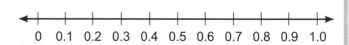

_____ = _____ = _____

3 Make a sum of a whole number and a number less than 1.

$\frac{5}{4}$

4 Show $\frac{33}{100}$ on the number line.

0   0.1   0.2   0.3   0.4   0.5   0.6   0.7   0.8   0.9   1.0

THURSDAY Geometry

1 Draw and label a line.

2 Name a quadrilateral that has:
- four sides of equal length
- four right angles

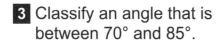
_____

3 Classify an angle that is between 70° and 85°.

A. acute   B. right   C. obtuse

4 What fraction of a turn is this angle?

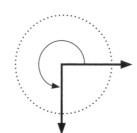

A. $\frac{1}{4}$ turn

B. $\frac{3}{4}$ turn

C. 1 full turn

D. $\frac{1}{2}$ turn

1 Complete the table.

Meters	Centimeters
1	100
2	
3	
4	

2 How many years in a millennium?

3 Abdullah has 1 quart of milk in one jug and 1 pint of milk in another jug. Can he pour the milk from both jugs into a third jug that has a capacity of 1 gallon? Justify your answer.

4 a) Explain how to find the perimeter of the shape.
b) Calculate the perimeter.

9 ft.

BRAIN STRETCH

At the Northland Science Reserve, small farm animals feed and play in a field measuring 40 yards by 10 yards.

a) What is the area of the field in yards?
b) What is the perimeter of the field in feet?
c) If each yard of fencing costs $10, how much will it cost to buy a new fence for the field?

MONDAY — Operations and Algebraic Thinking

1 Ted had 12 balloons at his party. At her party, Julia wants to have 3 times as many balloons as Ted did. Which equation shows the number of balloons Julia should buy?

A. 3 × 12 = 36
B. 3 + 12 = 15
C. 3 × 12 = 30

2 Josh took out 3 books from the library. The next day he took out 2 more. Write an expression that shows how many books Josh took out altogether.

3 Label the numbers as prime (P) or composite (C).

A. 15 _____
B. 6 _____
C. 90 _____

4 Extend the pattern.

20, 40, 80, _____, _____, _____

What is the rule? _____

TUESDAY — Operations in Base Ten

1 6 tens = _____ ones

2 Write the number in standard form.

40,000 + 6,000 + 200 + 20 + 7

= _____

3 What number is 1,000 more than 79,833?

4 Draw a model to find the quotient. Is there a remainder?

12 ÷ 3 =

WEDNESDAY — Fractions

1 Draw a model to show that 0.4 < 0.5.

2 Complete the equivalent fraction.

$$\frac{4}{10} = \frac{}{100}$$

3 Compare the fractions using >, <, or =.

$$\frac{2}{4} \quad \boxed{} \quad \frac{2}{8}$$

4 Write the fraction as a decimal.

$$\frac{42}{100} =$$

THURSDAY — Geometry

1 Draw and label a line segment.

2 Describe the polygon.

Name _____

Number of obtuse angles _____

Number of acute angles _____

3 What fraction of a turn is this angle?

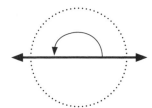

A. $\frac{1}{4}$ turn

B. $\frac{3}{4}$ turn

C. 1 full turn

D. $\frac{1}{2}$ turn

4 Classify an angle that is 90°.

A. acute   B. right   C. obtuse

1 If 1 foot is 1 inch, then

2 feet is ____ inches and

3 feet is ____ inches.

2 Evan started his homework at 8:15 p.m. and finished at 9:18 p.m. How long did Evan's homework take?

3 Sara got $20 for her birthday. She put $5 in her piggy bank, she spent $4 on candy, and she gave $2 to her brother. How much money does she have left?

4 Shade in a shape with a perimeter of 8 units. What is the area of your shape?

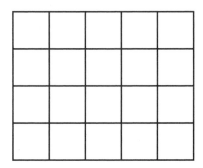

BRAIN STRETCH

Amelia is designing a flower bed. Her first design is a rectangle 12 feet long and 9 feet wide. Her second design is a square that has the same perimeter as the rectangle. Do both designs have the same area? Justify your answer.

1 Write a multiplication expression for the statement.

5 times as many as ◆◆◆◆◆◆◆◆

2 Write the first 5 terms of this pattern:

Start at 800 and add by 20 each time.

_____, _____, _____, _____, _____

3 On a trip, Dan's family travels 164 miles the first day, 39 miles the second day, and 193 miles the third day.

a) Estimate the miles driven. Explain.

b) Calculate the total miles.

4 Tim's team won 3 games in a baseball tournament. Ben's team won 3 times as many games as Tim's team. Find the number of games won by Ben's team. Use the tape diagram to solve the problem.

t is Tim's wins   *b* is Ben's wins

| 3 wins |

| 3 wins | 3 wins | 3 wins |

$3 \times t = b$

$3 \times \underline{\quad} = \underline{\quad}$

TUESDAY — Operations in Base Ten

1 Compare using >, <, or =.

153,431 ☐ 152,431

2 Round 4,250 to the nearest thousand. Draw a number line to help decide if 4,250 is closer to 4000 or 5000.

3 Make the greatest possible number with these digits.

7 3 1 4 6 9

_____

4
```
   7,865
+    391
```

WEDNESDAY   Fractions

1 Jake says 0.21 is greater than 0.6 Do you agree? Use words and a picture to justify your answer.

3 Write the fraction as a decimal.

$$\frac{9}{10} =$$

4 Michelle cut a pie into 8 equal pieces. She gave one piece to her cousin. What fraction of the pie did Michelle have left? Draw a model to show your work.

2 a) To create equivalent fractions, multiply the numerator and the denominator by the _____ number.

b) Fill in the boxes for equivalent fractions.

$$\frac{1}{2} \qquad \frac{2}{4} = \frac{2 \times \square}{2 \times \square} \qquad \frac{3}{6} = \frac{3 \times \square}{3 \times \square}$$

THURSDAY   Geometry

1 Draw and label line segment *GH*. Draw a point *P* on it.

2 Draw an acute angle. Label it *ABC*.

3 How many lines of symmetry?

X _____

4 Describe the polygon.

Name _____

Number of obtuse angles _____

Number of acute angles _____

Josh recorded the colors of cars in the Super Mart parking lot. Complete the bar graph using the data he collected.

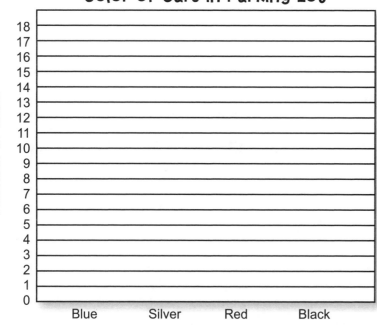

Color of Cars in Parking Lot

Number of Cars (y-axis: 0–18)

Colors (x-axis: Blue, Silver, Red, Black)

Color	Number
Blue	17
Silver	7
Red	13
Black	6

1 How many more silver cars were there than black cars? _____

2 How many more black cars would be needed to make 12 black cars altogether?

_____

3 How many cars were in the parking lot altogether? _____

BRAIN STRETCH

The workers in a toy factory can manufacture 38 teddy bears in an hour.

a) How many teddy bears can they make in 40 hours?
b) One quarter of the teddy bears are brown and the rest are white.
   How many teddy bears of each color will the workers have made in 40 hours?

MONDAY — Operations and Algebraic Thinking

1 Solve for *x*.

$5x = 25$ $x =$ _____

2 David has 85 CDs. His mother bought him *c* more CDs. Write an expression that shows how many CDs David has now.

3 Find the missing number in the sequence.

200, 175, _____, 125, 100

4 Predict the 21st figure in this pattern.

A. 🚲   B. 🚑   C. 🚒

TUESDAY — Operations in Base Ten

1 9 hundreds = _____ tens

2 Order the numbers from least to greatest.

10,322   10,300   10,364

_____ < _____ < _____

3 Complete the model to find the product of 23 × 12.

	10	2
20	10 × 20 = 200	___ × ___ = ___
3	___ × ___ = ___	___ × ___ = ___

200 + ____ + ____ + ____ = ____

4 $98.45
    − $13.37
    _____

WEDNESDAY Fractions

1 Jack used a 6 × 6 grid to represent 1 and Emma used a 3 × 3 grid to represent 1. Each student shaded grid squares to show $\frac{1}{3}$.

a) How many squares did each one shade?

Jack: _____ Emma _____

b) Why did they shade different numbers of grid squares?

3 Write the fraction as a decimal.

$$\frac{7}{100} =$$

2 Compare the fractions using >, <, or =.

$$\frac{3}{6} \boxed{} \frac{3}{12}$$

4 Dave hiked $1\frac{1}{2}$ miles one day and twice that far the next day.

a) Draw a model to show $2 × 1\frac{1}{2}$.
b) How far did Dave hike altogether?

THURSDAY Geometry

1 Draw an obtuse angle. Label it *EFG*.

2 Draw an 80° angle. Classify the angle.

3 Classify the following pair of lines.

A. intersecting

B. parallel

C. perpendicular

4 Look at the shapes. Choose flip, slide, or turn.

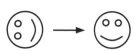

A. flip   B. slide   C. turn

1 Complete the table.

Yards	Feet
1	3
2	
3	
4	

2 Charlotte jogs 8 kilometers a day, 6 days a week. How many meters does Charlotte cover in 1 year?
Hint: 1 km = 1,000 m

3 Each week Leo plays soccer for 270 minutes. What is Leo's playing time in hours and minutes? Complete the table to help you.

Hours	Minutes
1	60
2	
3	
4	
5	

4 Find the perimeter and the area of the shaded shape.

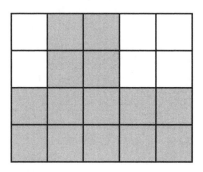

Perimeter = _____ units

Area = _____ square units

BRAIN STRETCH

Mrs. Kumar wants to buy cupcakes for the grade 4 classes. The cupcakes are sold in boxes of 6. Each class has 23 students and there are 4 classes in total.
How many boxes of cupcakes should Mrs. Kumar buy? Is your answer reasonable? Explain your thinking.

Operations and Algebraic Thinking

1 Write a multiplication expression

2 times as many as

◆◆◆◆◆◆◆◆◆◆

2 Write the first 5 terms of this pattern:

Start at 2 and multiply by 3 each time.

_____, _____, _____, _____, _____

3 Label the numbers as prime (P) or composite (C).

A. 25 _____

B. 99 _____

C. 3 _____

4 Helen needs 5 times as many cups of milk as eggs for her recipe. If she uses 5 eggs, how many cups of milk will she need? Draw a model to find the answer.

TUESDAY
Operations in Base Ten

1 What is the value of the underlined digit?

<u>6</u>73,204 _____

2 Round the number to the nearest hundred.

129,455 _____

3 If 8 × 14 = 112, what is 7 × 14?

4
    2,870
  + 6,684

1 Use a model to show that $\frac{1}{4} = \frac{2}{8}$.

2 Complete the sums.

$$\frac{5}{10} = \frac{1}{10} + \frac{}{10} + \frac{}{10}$$

$$\frac{5}{10} = \frac{2}{10} + \frac{}{10}$$

3 Compare the fractions using >, < , or =.

$$\frac{2}{4} \ \boxed{} \ \frac{1}{2}$$

4 Valerie says 0.55 is less than 0.2. Do you agree? Use words and a picture to justify your answer.

THURSDAY — Geometry

1 Draw a right angle. Label it *JKL*.

2 Draw and label line segment *MN*. Draw a point *X* on it.

3 Classify an angle that is 150°.

A. obtuse   B. right   C. acute

4 Name a quadrilateral that has:
• opposite sides equal
• four right angles

_____

1 12 L = _____ mL

2 How many years in 4 decades?

3 Joanna bought a bag of cherries for $2.86. She paid $10.00. How much change did Joanna receive?

4 Find the perimeter and the area of the rectangle.

12 yd.

7 yd.

Perimeter = ____ yd.

Area = ____ square yd.

BRAIN STRETCH

This season, Barbara's hockey team won 12 games and lost 3 games.

a) How many games did the team play altogether?

b) If it costs $3 to watch each game, how much did Barbara's mother pay to watch all the games this season?

c) Barbara's hockey team will play three times as many games next year. How many games will the team play?

MONDAY — Operations and Algebraic Thinking

1 Solve for *b*.

$50 \div b = 10$ $b =$ _____

2 Leo collected $10 for a school fundraiser. Cameron collected 5 times as much money as Leo. Which expression represents the amount of money Cameron collected?

A. 5 + 5   B. 5 + 10   C. 5 × 10

3 Extend the pattern.

2, 4, 8, 16, _____, _____

What is the rule? _____

_____

4 Draw the 11th shape in this pattern.

TUESDAY — Operations in Base Ten

1 3 hundreds = _____ ones

2 Compare using >, <, or =.

455,601 ☐ 355,621

3 Write 17,400 in words.

_____

_____

_____

_____

4 Draw a model to find the quotient. Is there a remainder?

$26 \div 8 =$

1 Write the fraction that names the shaded part.

2 Complete the equivalent fraction.

$$\frac{5}{10} = \frac{}{100}$$

3 Compare the fractions using >, <, or =.

$$\frac{1}{3} \boxed{} \frac{1}{30}$$

4 Subtract.

$$\frac{6}{7} - \frac{1}{7} =$$

THURSDAY   Geometry

1 Draw and label a set of perpendicular lines.

2 Classify the angle as acute, obtuse, or right.

3 Find the unknown angle measure.

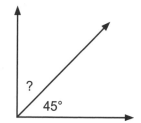

? 45°

4 Which shape is **not** a quadrilateral?

A. octagon

B. rhombus

C. square

1 10 pints = _____ cups

2 How many hours in a day?

3 Sunita's parents want to drive to the next town to visit family. The trip takes an hour and a half. If they leave at 8:30 a.m., will they get there by 10:15 a.m.? Use the number line to show your work.

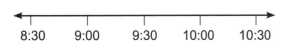

8:30   9:00   9:30   10:00   10:30

4 Find the perimeter and the area of the shaded shape.

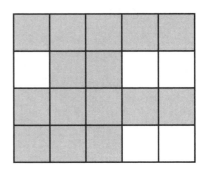

Perimeter = _____ units

Area = _____ square units

BRAIN STRETCH

List five ways you use math every day.

MONDAY — Operations and Algebraic Thinking

1 Complete the fact family.

$5 \times 8 = 40$ ___ $\times$ ___ $= 40$

___ $\div$ ___ $=$ ___   ___ $\div$ ___ $=$ ___

2 Fill in the blank to make the equation true.

$64 \div$ ____ $= 8$

3 Here is Lisa's pattern:

When Lisa has drawn 8 stars, how many octagons will she have in her pattern?

4 a) Find the missing number in the sequence.

800, 725, 650, 575, _____, 425

b) What do you notice about the numbers?

TUESDAY — Operations in Base Ten

1 What is the value of the underlined digit?

1̲57,963 _____

2 Write the numeral 378,674 in expanded form.

_____

_____

_____

3 Round the number to the place of the underlined digit.

2̲1,678 _____

4 Draw a model to find the quotient. Is there a remainder?

$16 \div 5 =$

WEDNESDAY Fractions

1 There are 2 pizzas that are the same size. One pizza has $\frac{1}{2}$ left. The other pizza has $\frac{5}{8}$ left. Which pizza has more left? Use an area model to show your work.

2 Compare the fractions using >, < , or =. Use a number line to show your work.

$\frac{3}{9}$ ☐ $\frac{1}{4}$

3 Write the fraction as a decimal.

$\frac{99}{100}$ =

4 Look at this sum of fractions:

$\frac{4}{6} = \frac{1}{6} + \frac{1}{6} + \frac{2}{6}$

Write a different sum of fractions with the same denominator:

$\frac{4}{6}$ =

THURSDAY Geometry

1 Draw and label ray *DE*. Draw a point *B* on it.

2 Draw a 45° angle. Classify the angle.

3 What is the measure of ∠*ABC*?

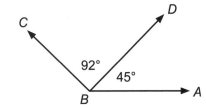

4 Look at the shapes. Choose flip, slide, or turn.

A. flip   B. slide   C. turn

Measurement and Data

Time Spent Studying Spelling Words

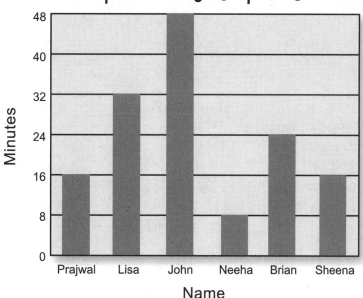

1 How many students were surveyed? _____

2 What is the range of the data? _____

3 Who spent the most time studying spelling words? _____

4 For how many minutes did Neeha and Prajwal study altogether? _____

5 How many more minutes did John spend studying than Sheena? _____

BRAIN STRETCH

One orange costs $0.60 or you can buy a dozen for $5.99.

a) Which is the better buy? Justify your answer.

b) If you bought a dozen oranges and used $10 to pay
   for your them, what would your change be?

Operations and Algebraic Thinking

1 Find the missing factor.

6 × _____ = 42

2 Label the numbers as prime (P) or composite (C).

A. 77 _____

B. 16 _____

C. 29 _____

3 You have 2 bags of oranges and there are 10 oranges in each bag. How many oranges are there altogether? Draw a model or use an equation to find the answer.

4 Create a growing pattern using numbers. Write the pattern rule and the first five terms.

Rule: _____

_____, _____, _____ , _____, _____

Operations in Base Ten

1 700 tens = _____ ones

2 Round the number to the nearest hundred.

982,397 _____

3 Write 178,900 in words.

_____

_____

_____

_____

4 Divide. Use words, pictures, or equations to show your work.

400 ÷ 4 =

WEDNESDAY Fractions

1 Complete the equivalent fraction.

$$\frac{7}{10} = \frac{}{100}$$

2 Put the fractions in order from least to greatest. Use a model to show your work.

$$\frac{4}{5} \qquad \frac{1}{5} \qquad \frac{3}{5}$$

3 Compare the decimals using <, >, or =.

0.40 ☐ 0.04

4 Use the model to help complete the statements.

$$\frac{1}{2} + \frac{1}{2} + \frac{1}{2} = 3 \times \underline{}$$

$$3 \times \frac{1}{2} = \underline{}$$

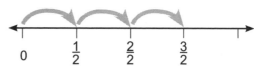

THURSDAY Geometry

1 Draw and label a set of parallel lines.

2 Classify the angle as acute, obtuse, or right.

3 Describe the polygon.

Name _____

Number of obtuse angles _____

Number of acute angles _____

4 Circle the figures that are congruent.

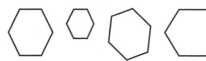

1 200 m = _____ cm

2 How many days in a year?

3 Astrid bought a smoothie for $1.42. She paid with $2.00. What are two combinations of coins that Astrid could receive as change? What is the fewest number of coins she could receive?

4 How many 1-foot squares of carpet are needed to cover the floor?

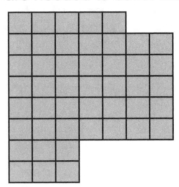

 1-foot square

BRAIN STRETCH

Melissa's family is traveling to Lewistown by train to see her aunt.

a) If each car is 11 m long and there are 9 cars in the train, how many meters long is the train?

b) Each car can hold 48 passengers. How many people can ride on the train at one time?

c) If the train left at 9 a.m. and the trip takes 7 hours, when will Melissa and her family arrive in Lewiston?

MONDAY — Operations and Algebraic Thinking

1 You have 15 slices of pizza. If 5 people want to share the pizza equally, how many slices should each person get? Draw a model or use an equation to find the answer.

2 Write an equation to describe the output rule. Complete the table.

Rule: _____

Input	x	2	4	6	8	10
Output	y	10	20	30		

3 List all of the prime numbers between 2 and 15.

4 Compare the expressions using <, >, or =.

5×6 ☐ $(6 \times 6) + 4$

TUESDAY — Operations in Base Ten

1 9 hundred thousands

= _____ hundreds

2 Round the number to the nearest ten thousand.

672,928 _____

3 Draw a model to find the quotient. Is there a remainder?

$25 \div 5 =$

4
```
  6,605
− 3,291
```

WEDNESDAY — Fractions

1 Write the fraction that names the shaded part.

2 Complete the equivalent fraction.

$$\frac{6}{10} = \frac{\quad}{100}$$

3 Compare the fractions using >, < , or =.

$$\frac{7}{8} \;\boxed{}\; \frac{9}{11}$$

4 Add.

$$\frac{4}{10} + \frac{20}{100} = \frac{\quad}{100}$$

THURSDAY — Geometry

1 Draw a 30° angle. Classify the angle.

2 Describe the polygon.

Name _____

Number of obtuse angles _____

Number of acute angles _____

3 How many lines of symmetry?

K _____

4 What fraction of a turn is this angle?

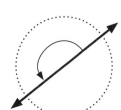

A. $\frac{1}{4}$ turn

B. $\frac{3}{4}$ turn

C. 1 full turn

D. $\frac{1}{2}$ turn

1 15 minutes = _____ seconds

6 hours = _____ minutes

2 quarter hours = _____ minutes

2 Toby purchased two pairs of socks for $7.50. He paid with two $5 bills. How much change did Toby receive?

3 Find the perimeter of the equilateral triangle.

8 ft.

4 What are the perimeter and area of a square garden with sides 7 meters?

Perimeter = _____

Area = _____

BRAIN STRETCH

Last year Claire planted 6 rows of tulips in her garden. Each row had 9 tulip bulbs. This year she planted 70 tulip bulbs. Her goal is to have 300 tulips altogether.

a) How many more tulips should Claire plant next year?

b) Is your answer reasonable?
c) Explain your thinking.

Operations and Algebraic Thinking

1 Write a multiplication expression for the statement.

7 times as many as ◆◆◆

2 Fill in the blank to make the equation true.

$55 \div 11 = \underline{\hspace{1cm}} \div 4$

3 Kevin had $90. He bought two CDs for $18 and a T-shirt for $11. What would be a reasonable estimate of how much money he has left over? Describe how you came up with your estimate.

4 Create an ABB pattern by coloring.

OOOOOOOOOO

TUESDAY

Operations in Base Ten

1 Compare using >, <, or =.

567,103 $\boxed{}$ 9,567,103

2 If 6 × 139 = 834, what is 7 × 139?

3
```
    3,784
 +    430
```

4 Write the number in standard form.

1,000,000 + 300,000 + 70,000 + 2,000 + 10 + 3

= _____

WEDNESDAY — Fractions

1 a) Complete the pattern of equivalent fractions.

$$\frac{1}{2} = \frac{2}{4} = \frac{3}{6} = \frac{4}{8} = \frac{5}{}$$

b) What rule did you use?

2 Draw a model to show an equivalent fraction for $\frac{6}{9}$.

3 Put the fractions in order from least to greatest.
Draw a model to show your work.

$$\frac{3}{7} \qquad \frac{1}{7} \qquad \frac{5}{7}$$

4 Write the fraction as a decimal.

$$\frac{2}{10} =$$

THURSDAY — Geometry

1 Draw and label line segment *AB*.
Draw a point *D* on it.

2 Classify an angle that is between 30° and 60°.

A. acute   B. right   C. obtuse

3 Draw a 160° angle.
Classify the angle.

4 Circle the figures that are similar.

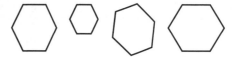

Pop Tabs Collected Each Month

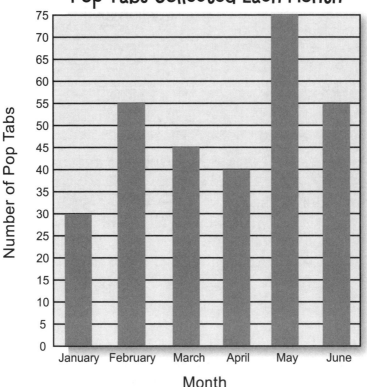

Number of Pop Tabs vs Month

1 In which month were the fewest pop tabs collected? _____

2 In which month were the most pop tabs collected? _____

3 How many fewer pop tabs were collected in January than June? _____

4 What is the difference in the number of pop tabs collected in February and May? _____

5 What is the mode of the data? _____

BRAIN STRETCH

Mei Ling divided 87 jelly beans equally into 6 bags. She gave away all but 1 bag and the leftover jelly beans. How many jelly beans did she keep?

MONDAY Operations and Algebraic Thinking

1 Write a multiplication expression for the statement.

8 times as many as ◆◆◆◆◆◆

2 List all of the factor pairs of 30.

3 A garden has 8 rows with 7 tomato plants in each row. Write an equation for the total number of tomato plants in the garden. Let *y* represent the total number of tomato plants.

4 Extend the pattern.

11, 22, 33, 44, _____, _____

What is the rule? ________________

____

TUESDAY Operations in Base Ten

1 6 hundred thousands

= ____ ten thousands

2 Round the number to the nearest ten.

528,725 ____________________

3 Draw a model to find the quotient. Is there a remainder?

$14 \div 4 =$

4

$$\begin{array}{r} 8{,}782 \\ +\ 1{,}562 \\ \hline \end{array}$$

1 Complete the equivalent fraction.

$$\frac{6}{7} = \frac{12}{\underline{\hspace{1em}}}$$

2 Write an equivalent fraction.
Use the smallest numbers you can.

$$\frac{6}{8} = $$

3 Add.

$$\frac{2}{10} + \frac{78}{100} = \frac{}{100}$$

4 Write $3\frac{1}{6}$ as a sum of fractions.
Draw a model to show your work.

THURSDAY — Geometry

1 Draw a 50° angle. Classify the angle.

2 What is the measure of $\angle RST$?

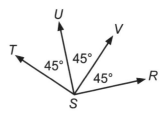

3 Name a quadrilateral that has two pairs of parallel sides

_____

4 Are these shapes congruent or similar?

1 Draw a line 25 mm long.

2 Marlene's mom lets her play video games for 30 minutes every night. How many hours does she spend playing video games in 2 weeks?

3 A car left Oaktown and traveled for 3 hours and 25 minutes to Sprucetown. Then the car traveled for 1 hour and 35 minutes and arrived in Pinetown at 1:30 p.m. What time did the car leave Oaktown?

4 Find the perimeter of the trapezoid.

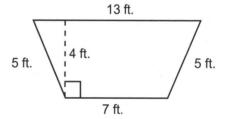

BRAIN STRETCH

Madelyn wants to buy 4 bunches of tulips. Each bunch costs $3.60. She pays with a $20 bill. Estimate how much change she should get. Then calculate the exact change.

1 Circle the multiples of 7.

49   63   100   70

2 Find the missing number in the sequence.

9, 18, 27, _____, 45, 54, 63

3 Green mitts cost $7. Black mitts cost three times as much as the green mitts. How much do the black mitts cost? Use the tape diagram to help solve.

g is the cost of green mitts
b is the cost of black mitts

$7

$7	$7	$7

$3 \times g = b$

$3 \times$ ___ = ___

4 Write an equation to describe the output rule. Complete the table.

Rule: _____

Input	x	1	2	3	4	5
Output	y	5	10	15		

1

$$\begin{array}{r} \$154.76 \\ -\ \$\ 13.40 \\ \hline \end{array}$$

2 Round the number to the nearest hundred thousand.

983,266 _____

3 Use the expanded form of a number to multiply it.

$473 \times 4 = ($ _____ $\times\ 4) + ($ _____ $\times\ 4) + ($ _____ $\times\ 4)$

=

WEDNESDAY   Fractions

1 Write an equivalent fraction.

$$\frac{3}{7} =$$

2 Put the fractions in order from greatest to least. Draw a model to show your work.

$$\frac{1}{2} \qquad \frac{3}{4} \qquad \frac{1}{4}$$

3 Add.

$$\frac{10}{100} + \frac{5}{10} = \frac{}{10}$$

4 Draw a model to multiply the fraction.

$$\frac{2}{3} \times 5 =$$

THURSDAY   Geometry

1 Classify the angle as acute, obtuse, or right.

2 Draw a 20° angle. Classify the angle.

3 How many parallel sides does a rhombus have?

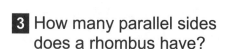

4 Look at the shapes. Choose flip, slide, or turn.

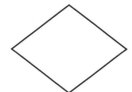

A. flip   B. slide   C. turn

Measurement and Data

Spelling Test Results

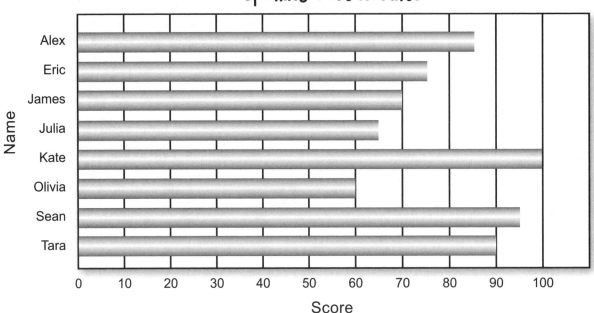

1 Who got 100 on the spelling test? _____

2 Which student(s) got a score between 60 and 80? _____

3 What is the range of the test scores? _____

4 What is the difference between James's and Sean's scores? _____

5 What is the mean score? _____

6 Who got 60 on the spelling test? _____

BRAIN STRETCH

A jug has a volume of 4 cups.
Is the volume of 4 jugs less than 2 pints?
Write an expression and solve.
Let *j* represent the volume of the jug.

Operations and Algebraic Thinking

1 Complete the fact family.

$$7 \times 4 = 28 \qquad \underline{} \times \underline{} = 28$$

$$\underline{} \div \underline{} = \underline{} \qquad \underline{} \div \underline{} = \underline{}$$

2 Fill in the blank to make the equation true.

$$8 \times \underline{} = 68 - 4$$

3 Write the first 5 terms of this pattern:

Start at 4 and multiply by 10 each time.

$$\underline{}, \underline{}, \underline{}, \underline{}, \underline{}$$

4 This week, Jade practiced the piano for 75 minutes. She practiced for three times as long as Lauren did. How many minutes did Lauren spend practicing the piano? Write an equation to help you solve this problem.

Operations in Base Ten

1 Round the number to the place of the underlined digit.

7<u>8</u>9,444 _____

2 Order the numbers from least to greatest.

88,791   77,918   77,911

_____ < _____ < _____

3 If 5 × 5 = 25, what is 15 × 5?

4 Multiply. Use words, pictures, or equations to show your work.

19 × 15 =

WEDNESDAY — Fractions

1 Complete the equivalent fraction.

$$\frac{4}{5} = \frac{16}{\rule{1cm}{0.4pt}}$$

2 Write an equivalent fraction. Use the smallest numbers you can.

$$\frac{3}{12} =$$

3 Add.

$$\frac{1}{10} + \frac{60}{100} = \frac{}{10}$$

4 Multiply. Draw a model to show your work.

$$3 \times \frac{1}{3} =$$

THURSDAY — Geometry

1 Draw and label a set of intersecting lines.

2 How many right angles does a rectangle have?

3 Draw a line of symmetry.

4 Classify the triangle.

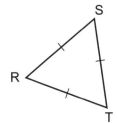

A. acute

B. isosceles

C. obtuse

D. equilateral

E. scalene

Measurement and Data

Construct a horizontal bar graph using the information from the table.

Number of Books Read

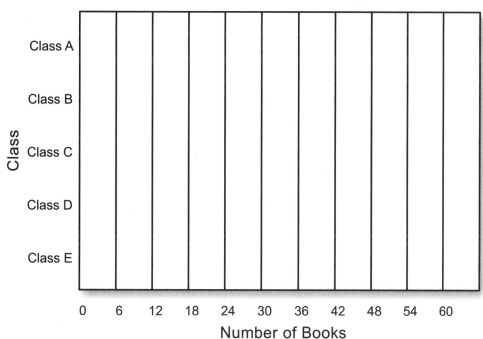

Class	Number of Books
Class A	54
Class B	42
Class C	48
Class D	36
Class E	60

1 Which class read the most books? _____

2 If each student in Class C read 2 books, how many students are in Class C? _____

3 Which class read the fewest books? _____

4 List the classes from the class that read the most books to the class that read the fewest books. _____

5 How many classes read more than 48 books? _____

BRAIN STRETCH

A jar holds 500 mL of jam. A carton holds 4 jars.
How many jars and cartons are needed to package 6.5 L of jam?

MONDAY — Operations and Algebraic Thinking

1 Corey rides the bus 4 times more often than Jane. Let *j* represent the number of times Jane rides the bus. Write an expression to show how often Corey rides the bus.

2 Write an equation to describe the output rule. Complete the table.

Rule: _____

Input	x	6	12	18	24	30
Output	y	1	7	13		

3 Complete the pattern.

$9 \times 9 = 81$

$9 \times 90 = $ _____

$9 \times 900 = $ _____

$9 \times 9{,}000 = $ _____

4 Compare the expressions using <, >, or =.

$(20 - 10) \times 6$ ☐ $50 + 10$

TUESDAY — Operations in Base Ten

1 _____ tens = 2,000 ones

2 Write 24,671 in words.

_____

_____

3
$$9{,}673$$
$$- 5{,}783$$

4 Divide. 112 ÷ 7. Complete the model to show your work.

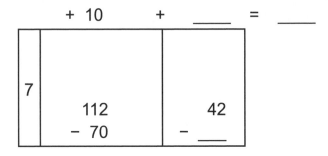

WEDNESDAY Fractions

1 Write an equivalent fraction. Use the smallest numbers you can.

$$\frac{10}{30} =$$

2 Add. Simplify your answer.

$$\frac{1}{4} + \frac{1}{4} =$$

3 Draw a model to multiply the fraction.

$$\frac{2}{3} \times 5 =$$

4 There are 24 apples in a basket. If $\frac{1}{4}$ are green, how many green apples are there? Draw a model to show your reasoning.

THURSDAY Geometry

1 Draw a 120° angle. Classify the angle.

2 What is the sum of the angles in *PQRS*?

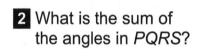
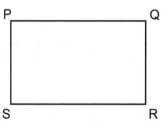

3 Describe the polygon.

Name _____

Number of obtuse angles _____

Number of acute angles _____

4 Are these shapes congruent or similar?

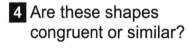

Eleni practices piano every day. Here is some data about her practice time.

Time Spent Practicing Piano Each Day

$\frac{1}{4}$ hour	$\frac{3}{4}$ hour	$\frac{1}{4}$ hour	$\frac{1}{2}$ hour
$\frac{1}{2}$ hour	$\frac{3}{4}$ hour	$\frac{3}{4}$ hour	$\frac{1}{4}$ hour
$\frac{1}{2}$ hour	$\frac{3}{4}$ hour	$\frac{1}{2}$ hour	$\frac{3}{4}$ hour

1 Create a line plot to represent the data.

2 Which was the most frequent time interval? _____

3 For how many minutes did Eleni practice piano over the last 12 days? _____

BRAIN STRETCH

The difference between two mixed numbers is $2\frac{1}{4}$.
What are possible combinations of the two mixed numbers?
List as many different solutions as you can.

1 List all of the factor pairs of 72.

2 Gina rides her bike 4 kilometers every day. How many days will it take her to ride her bike 32 kilometers? Write an equation to help you solve this problem.

3 Create a shrinking pattern using numbers. Write the pattern rule and the first five terms.

Rule: _____

_____ , _____ , _____ , _____ , _____

4 Compare the expressions using <, >, or =.

$(2 + 6) \times 5$ ⬚ 3×10

1 5 hundreds = _____ ones

2 Round the number to the nearest ten.

451,763 _____

3 Complete the pattern.

$18 \div 3 = 6$

$180 \div 3 =$ _____

$1,800 \div 3 =$ _____

4 If $8 \times 5 = 40$, what is 16×5?

WEDNESDAY Fractions

1 Complete the equivalent fraction.

$$\frac{3}{10} = \frac{}{100}$$

2 Write an equivalent fraction.
Use the smallest numbers you can.

$$\frac{21}{24} =$$

3 Add.

$$\frac{20}{100} + \frac{3}{10} = \frac{}{10}$$

4 Draw a model to multiply the fraction.

$$\frac{2}{5} \times 3 =$$

THURSDAY Geometry

1 Draw an isosceles triangle.
Measure and label the angles.

2 What is a straight angle?

3 Name a quadrilateral that has
exactly one pair of parallel sides

_____

4 Find the unknown angle measure.

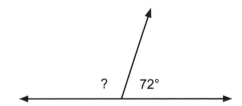

? 72°

1 70 lb. = _____ oz.

2 About how much tea does a cup hold?

    A. 1 L   B. 1 mL   C. 250 mL

3 Steven brushes his teeth twice a day for 2 minutes each time. How many minutes does he spend brushing his teeth in 4 weeks?

4 Calculate the perimeter.

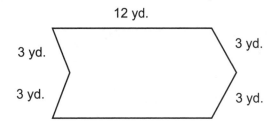

BRAIN STRETCH

Leonard delivers newspapers daily to 21 houses on Main Street, 16 houses on Elm Street, and 34 houses on Lincoln Avenue. If Leonard delivers a total of 120 papers per day, how many papers does he have left to deliver after he visits those three streets?

1 Write the related multiplication and division sentences to complete the fact family.

6 × 9 = 54

2 Manny collected $6 for a school fundraiser. Kelly collected $48 for the fundraiser. How many times as much money did Kelly collect compared to Manny?

3 Find the missing number in the sequence.

0.5, 1, 1.5, 2, _____, 3, 3.5

4 Circle the number that is **not** a multiple of 6.

12   24   36   40

1 Round the number to the place of the underlined digit.

2,225,6<u>8</u>1 _____

2 Order the numbers from greatest to least.

14,723   17,432   17,324

_____ > _____ > _____

3 Use the expanded form of a number to multiply it.

117 × 2 = (_____ × 2) + (_____ × 2) + (_____ × 2)

=

1 Write an equivalent fraction.

$$\frac{10}{12} =$$

2 Subtract.

$$\frac{5}{8} - \frac{2}{8} =$$

3 Draw a model to multiply the fraction.

$$\frac{2}{4} \times 4 =$$

4 Jose combined $\frac{3}{4}$ cup of oats, $\frac{1}{4}$ cup of raisins, and $\frac{1}{2}$ cup of nuts to make some trail mix. How much trail mix did he make?

THURSDAY | Geometry

1 Draw a 60° angle. Classify the angle.

2 Classify the triangle.
Circle all the descriptions that apply.

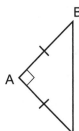

A. acute

B. isosceles

C. obtuse

D. equilateral

E. right

3 How many parallel sides does a right triangle have?

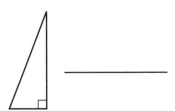 _____

4 How many lines of symmetry?

 _____

Monthly Rainfall

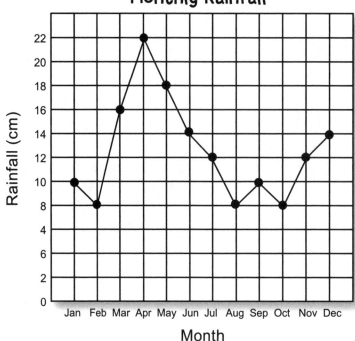

1 How much rain fell in May compared to February? _____

2 Which month had the most rainfall? _____

3 What was the range of the rainfall this year? _____

4 What was the rainfall in June? _____

5 How much rainfall was there in September and October? _____

BRAIN STRETCH

The sum of two mixed numbers is 6. What are possible combinations of the two mixed numbers? List as many different solutions as you can.

1 Write a multiplication expression for the statement.

6 times as many as ◆◆◆◆◆

2 There are 36 windows in a school. If each classroom has 3 windows, how many classrooms are there altogether? Write an equation to help you solve this problem.

3 What will be the 16th shape in this pattern?

4 Create a repeating pattern using the letters K, L, and O.

1 _____ tens = 40 ones

2 Compare using >, <, or =.

244,798 ☐ 9,304,798

3
```
  45,967
+ 34,861
```

4 Divide. Use words, pictures, or equations to show your work.

50 ÷ 4 =

WEDNESDAY — Fractions

1 Write an equivalent fraction. Use the smallest numbers you can.

$\dfrac{15}{63} =$

2 Look at this sum of fractions:

$\dfrac{4}{6} = \dfrac{1}{6} + \dfrac{1}{6} + \dfrac{2}{6}$

Write a different sum of fractions with the same denominator:

$\dfrac{4}{6} =$

3 Add. Simplify your answer.

$2\dfrac{1}{5} + 2\dfrac{2}{5} =$

4 Compare the decimals using <, >, or =.

0.33 ☐ 0.5

THURSDAY — Geometry

1 Draw and label a line *JK* that intersects a line *BC*.

2 Draw a 90° angle. Classify the angle.

3 Find the unknown angle measure.

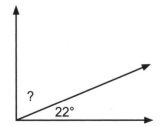

4 An equilateral triangle has

A. 3 sides that are the same length

B. 2 sides that are the same length

C. 3 sides of different lengths

1 7 years = _____ days

10 years = _____ months

2 How many meters in a kilometer?

3 Mrs. Martinez had $100 to spend on treats for the class party. She bought 8 boxes of drinks for $4 per box and 11 boxes of cupcakes for $6 per box. How much money did Mrs. Martinez have left over?

4 Calculate the perimeter and the area.

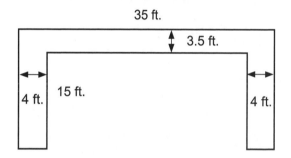

35 ft.

3.5 ft.

4 ft.   15 ft.   4 ft.

Perimeter = _____

Area = _____

BRAIN STRETCH

John had 1,268 marbles and gave his sister Barb half of them. If a tin holds 100 marbles, how many tins will Barb need to hold her marbles? Show your work.

1 Write the related multiplication and division sentences to complete the fact family.

$2 \times 19 = 38$

2 Scott picked 8 apples. Ann picked 32 apples. How many times more apples did Ann pick than Scott?

3 Circle the number that is **not** a multiple of 12?

144   48   56   36

4 Complete the pattern.

$5 \times 6 = 30$

$5 \times 60 = $ _____

$5 \times 600 = $ _____

$5 \times 6,000 = $ _____

TUESDAY — Operations in Base Ten

1 11 hundred thousands

= _____ ten thousands

2 Round the number to the nearest ten thousand.

685,812 _____

3
$$\begin{array}{r} 87,986 \\ + 19,634 \\ \hline \end{array}$$

4 Divide. Use words, pictures, or equations to show your work.

$32 \div 4 = $

1 Write an equivalent fraction.

$$\frac{7}{14} = $$

2 Add.

$$\frac{5}{10} + \frac{45}{100} = \frac{}{100}$$

3 Write the amount in decimal form.

forty-five hundredths

4 A punch recipe calls for $\frac{3}{8}$ of a cup of apple juice per person. There are 6 people. How many cups of apple juice are needed? Draw a model to show your reasoning.

1 Draw a 160° angle. Classify the angle.

2 What is the measure of ∠DGF?

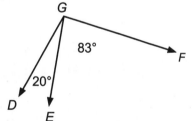

3 An acute triangle has

A. one 90° angle

B. one angle greater than 90°

C. all angles less than 90°

4 How many right angles does this trapezoid have? _____

Which line segments on the trapezoid are parallel? _____

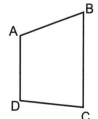

1 2 quarts = _____ pints

2 How many decades in a century?

3 Sophie's favorite CD has 10 songs on it. Its total running time is 39 minutes. On average, how many minutes long is each song?

4 Calculate the perimeter.

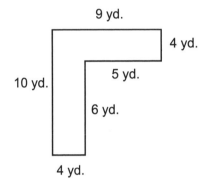

9 yd.

4 yd.

10 yd.

5 yd.

6 yd.

4 yd.

BRAIN STRETCH

In September, 67 students signed up for karate lessons. In October, 29 more students decided to join. Each karate class has a maximum of 8 students.

a) What is the least number of classes needed?

b) Is your answer reasonable?

c) Explain your thinking.

1 Compare the expressions using <, >, or =.

$(3 \times 2) + 3 \boxed{} 13 - 2$

2 List all of the factor pairs of 24.

3 A toy train costs $24. A toy car costs $6. Write two equations to show how many times as much the toy train costs as the toy car. Use multiplication in one equation and division in the other. Let *y* represent what you don't know.

4 Extend the pattern.

100, 80, 60, 40, _____, _____

What is the rule? _____

_____

TUESDAY — Operations in Base Ten

1 9 ten thousands

= _____ ones

2 Which digit is in the hundred thousands place?

521,683 _____

3 Multiply. Use words, pictures, or equations to show your work.

16 × 9 =

4 $250.82
    + $416.09

1 Write an improper fraction for the shaded parts.

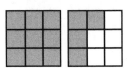

2 Compare the fractions using >, <, or =.

$$\frac{6}{10} \ \boxed{} \ \frac{6}{10}$$

3 Draw a model to multiply the fraction.

$$\frac{4}{7} \times 4 =$$

4 Henry practices playing his guitar for $\frac{2}{3}$ of an hour each day. How many hours does he practice in total after a week?

THURSDAY | Geometry

1 Draw and label a line *UV* parallel to a line *DE*.

2 Draw a 155° angle. Classify the angle.

3 Name a quadrilateral that has:
• two pairs of sides with equal length
• no parallel sides

_____

4 A right triangle has

A. one 90˚ angle

B. one angle greater than 90˚

C. all angles less than 90˚

Mr. Sullivan's students planted sunflowers in the school garden.
They measured the height of each sunflower after two weeks. Here is their data:

Heights of Sunflowers (inches)

$13\frac{1}{2}$ 13 $13\frac{3}{4}$ $13\frac{1}{4}$ $13\frac{3}{4}$ 14 $14\frac{1}{2}$ 14 $14\frac{1}{4}$ 14 $14\frac{3}{4}$ $13\frac{3}{4}$

1 How many sunflowers did the students plant? _____

2 Create a line plot to represent the data.

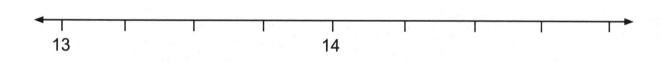

13   14

3 What is the difference in height between the tallest and shortest sunflowers?

_____

BRAIN STRETCH

Lillian ran 1.4 km on Monday, 1.8 km on Wednesday, and 2.1 km on Friday.

a) How many kilometers did she run altogether?
b) How much farther did she run on Friday than on Monday?

1 If there are 12 pencils in a box, how many pencils are in 11 boxes? Let p represent the number of pencils. Write an equation to help you find p.

_____ ☐ _____ = _____

p = _____

2 Circle the number that is **not** a multiple of 4.

31   36   48   16

3 Compare the expressions using <, >, or =.

20 ÷ 5 ☐ 10 + 10

4 What will be the 12th term in this pattern?

H S H S H S

1
```
   78,531
 −  2,567
```

2 Write the number in standard form.

100,000 + 50,000 + 3,000 + 80 + 7

= _____

3 Compare the 2 in the numbers 532 and 523. How is the value of 2 different in each number?

4 Divide. Use words, pictures, or equations to show your work.

33 ÷ 3 =

1 Write an improper fraction for the shaded parts.

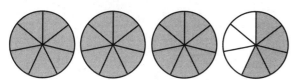

2 Add. Simplify your answer.

$$9\frac{1}{4} + 1\frac{1}{4} =$$

3 Compare the decimals using <, >, or =.

0.56 ☐ 0.97

4 A recipe calls for $\frac{1}{8}$ of a tablespoon of sugar per serving. How many tablespoons of sugar are needed to make 4 servings?

THURSDAY Geometry

1 Draw and label a line segment *FG* parallel to a line segment *PQ*.

2 Classify the angle as acute, obtuse, or right.

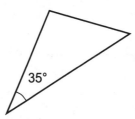

35°

3 Find the unknown angle measure.

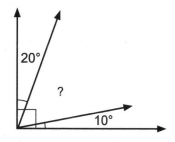

20°

?

10°

4 An isosceles triangle has

A. 3 sides that are the same length

B. 2 sides that are the same length

C. 3 sides of different lengths

Mr. Nag measured the growth of his tomato plant at the end of each week.

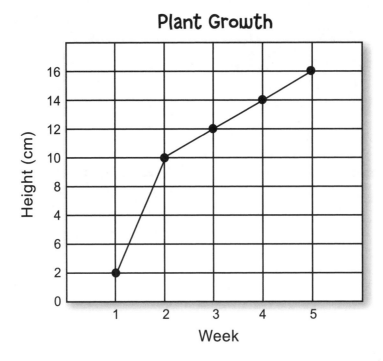

Plant Growth

1 How tall was the plant at the end of week 3? _____

2 How much did the plant grow from week 3 to week 4? _____

3 What was the height of the plant at the end of week 4? _____

4 What was the range of the height of the plant? _____

5 How much taller was the plant in week 4 than in week 2? _____

BRAIN STRETCH

If you had to build a tower with only one type of 3-D shape, what 3-D shape would you use? Why?

MONDAY — Operations and Algebraic Thinking

1 A giraffe is 18 feet tall.
He is 3 times as tall as a wallaby.
How tall is a wallaby?

2 Circle the multiples of 10.

60   72   100   20

3 Complete the pattern.

7 × 4 = 28

7 × 40 = _____

7 × 400 = _____

7 × 4,000 = _____

4 Create a repeating pattern using letters.
Write the pattern rule and the first five terms.

Rule: _____

_____ , _____, _____ , _____, _____

TUESDAY — Operations in Base Ten

1 Bill is 4th in line to get a drink.
There are 28 students in the line.
How many students are behind Bill?

2 Round the number to
the nearest hundred thousand.

428,755 _____

3 Which product is equivalent
to 10 × 600?

A. 10 × 6

B. 100 × 600

C. 6 × 1,000

4 Divide. Use words, pictures,
or equations to show your work.

220 ÷ 2 =

WEDNESDAY Fractions

1 Write an equivalent fraction. Use the smallest numbers you can.

$$\frac{16}{30} =$$

2 Write the fraction as a decimal.

$$\frac{50}{100} =$$

3 Subtract. Simplify your answer.

$$11\frac{3}{4} - 8\frac{1}{4} =$$

4 Multiply. Simplify your answer if you can.

$$\frac{2}{9} \times 7 =$$

THURSDAY Geometry

1 Draw and label a line *RS* perpendicular to a line *XY*.

2 Draw a 70° angle. Classify the angle.

3 Which triangle always has 3 acute angles and 3 sides the same length?

A. scalene

B. equilateral

C. isosceles

4 Are these shapes similar or congruent?

1 4 kg = _____ g

2 How many weeks in 5 years?

3 Pat's garden is a rectangle. It has an area of 60 square feet and is 5 feet wide. How long is the garden?

4 Which room has a larger area and perimeter? Justify your answer.

Room A: 10 ft. by 7 ft.

Room B: 6 ft. by 9 ft.

	Room A	Room B
Perimeter		
Area		

BRAIN STRETCH

Mr. Boyes needs to cook 7 pounds of potatoes for a party. He has $3\frac{1}{4}$ pounds of potatoes and his neighbor gives him another $2\frac{1}{4}$ pounds. How many more pounds of potatoes does Mr. Boyes need to buy?

Operations and Algebraic Thinking

1 If there are 68 rows in a theatre, and 33 seats in each row, estimate the total number of seats.

$68 \times 33 \approx$

2 Write an equation to describe the output rule. Complete the table.

Rule: _____

Input	x	9	8	7	6	5
Output	y	54	48	42		

3 List all the factor pairs for 77.

4 Dylan had 38 granola bars. He divided them equally among six friends and gave the leftovers away to his brother. How many bars did his friends get? How many bars did his brother get?

Operations in Base Ten

1 Compare using >, <, or =.

90,159 ☐ 90,159

2 Write the number in standard form.

$900,000 + 80,000 + 6,000 + 20 + 3$

= _____

3 Complete the pattern.

$32 \div 8 = 4$

$320 \div 8 =$ _____

$3,200 \div 8 =$ _____

4 Multiply. Use words, pictures, or equations to show your work.

$11 \times 11 =$

WEDNESDAY Fractions

1 Write the fraction as a decimal.

$$\frac{6}{10} =$$

2 Add.

$$\frac{8}{10} + \frac{52}{100} = \frac{}{100}$$

3 Subtract. Simplify your answer.

$$8\frac{11}{12} - 4\frac{9}{12} =$$

4 A recipe calls for $\frac{3}{4}$ of a cup of milk per serving. How many cups of milk are needed to make 6 servings?

THURSDAY Geometry

1 Draw a right triangle. Measure and label the angles.

2 Draw a quadrilateral that has:
• no sides parallel
• no sides perpendicular

3 A scalene triangle has

A. 3 sides that are the same length

B. 2 sides that are the same length

C. 3 sides of different lengths

4 Draw a line of symmetry.

1 10 yards = _____ feet

= _____ inches

2 How many pints in a gallon?

3 John delivers newspapers after dinner for 3.5 hours. If he starts at 6:15 p.m., when will he finish?

4 What are the perimeter and area of a tabletop with width 40 cm and length 100 cm?

Perimeter = _____

Area = _____

BRAIN STRETCH

At the fair, Demetra bought 9 six-packs of tickets to share with her two friends. Each ride costs 2 tickets. Are there enough tickets for each person to go on 6 rides? Justify your answer.

1 A sign at the grocery store says "Cucumbers, 2 for $4". You need 10 cucumbers. How much will 10 cucumbers cost?

2 What composite numbers are more than 40 but less than 45?

3 Peter has a sticker album. He puts 40 stamps on the first page, 46 on the second page, 52 on the third page, and 58 on the fourth page. If this pattern continues, how many stickers will Peter put on the sixth page? What is the rule for this pattern?

4 Write the first 5 terms of this pattern:

Start at 61 and add 11 each time.

____, ____, ____, ____, _____

TUESDAY — Operations in Base Ten

1 Round the number to the place of the underlined digit.

824,359 _____

2 By how many times is 300 greater than 30?

3 Multiply. Use words, pictures, or equations to show your work.

10 × 601 =

4
$$\begin{array}{r} 889{,}472 \\ -\ 355{,}177 \\ \hline \end{array}$$

WEDNESDAY — Fractions

1 Write an equivalent fraction. Use the smallest numbers you can.

$$\frac{9}{27} =$$

2 Add. Simplify your answer.

$$8\frac{1}{6} + 4\frac{3}{6} =$$

3 Write the amount in decimal form.

seven hundredths

4 Bessie made 4 pizzas and cut each of them into eighths. If she served $2\frac{3}{4}$ pizzas, how many slices of pizza did Bessie serve?

THURSDAY — Geometry

1 Draw and label a ray *CD* parallel to a line segment *UV*.

2 Which shape does **not** have four equal sides?

A. rhombus   B. rectangle   C. square

3 Write an equation to help you find ∠*POQ* and ∠*QOR*.

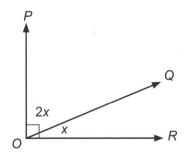

4 What fraction of a turn is this angle?

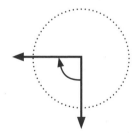

A. $\frac{1}{4}$ turn

B. $\frac{3}{4}$ turn

C. 1 full turn

D. $\frac{1}{2}$ turn

Week 25

At the Corner Cafe, the owner bakes one apple pie each day. He sells the pie by the slice. Each slice is $\frac{1}{8}$ of the pie.

These fractions show how much pie was left over each day this week:

$$\frac{1}{4} \qquad \frac{1}{2} \qquad \frac{3}{8} \qquad \frac{1}{8} \qquad \frac{1}{4} \qquad 0 \qquad \frac{1}{8}$$

1 Draw a line plot to represent the data.

0 $\frac{1}{2}$

2 On how many days was only 1 slice of pie left over? _____

3 If the owner takes home all the leftovers, how much apple pie did he take home over the week? Give your answer in two ways: number of pies and number of slices.

_____

BRAIN STRETCH

How could you measure the perimeter of a leaf?

Operations and Algebraic Thinking

1 Sam's class has a goal to collect 200 cans of food for a food drive. Sam brings in 3 packs with 6 cans of soup in each pack. Ellie brings in 5 packs with 6 cans. About how many cans still need to be collected? Explain your estimation strategy.

2 Compare the expressions using <, >, or =.

$30 \div 3$ ⬚ $(7 \times 3) - 3$

3 Mr. Freeman has a bag of 120 candies. He has 28 students and he wants to share the candies equally. How many candies should he give each student if he wants to have the fewest number of candies left over?

4 Create a growing geometric pattern using circles.

TUESDAY ## Operations in Base Ten

1 Round the number to the nearest thousand.

545,641 _____

2 Write the numeral 309,762 in expanded form.

_____

_____

_____

3 Order the numbers from least to greatest.

108,323   110,733   101,377

_____ < _____ < _____

4 Divide. Use words, pictures, or equations to show your work.

$77 \div 7 =$

WEDNESDAY — Fractions

1 Write the fraction as a decimal.

$$\frac{8}{10} =$$

2 Add. Simplify your answer.

$$3\frac{3}{9} + 5\frac{5}{9} =$$

3 Multiply. Simplify your answer if you can.

$$\frac{3}{6} \times 6 =$$

4 A factory puts $\frac{1}{3}$ of a gallon of chocolate syrup into each batch of ice cream. How many gallons of chocolate syrup will be used in 5 batches?

THURSDAY — Geometry

1 Draw and label line segment *ST*. Draw a point *H* on it.

2 Classify the angle as acute, obtuse, or right.

3 Classify the triangle. Circle all the descriptions that apply.

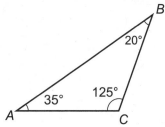

A. acute   D. equilateral

B. isosceles   E. right

C. obtuse

4 Find the unknown angle measure.

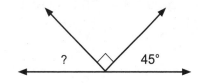

Mr. Capri's technology class recorded their typing speeds.
Here is a list of the number of words per minute each student can type:

Typing Speeds (words per minute)

| 12 | 16 | 11 | 12 | 14 | 20 | 11 | 19 | 17 | 11 | 17 | 12 | 16 | 18 | 12 | 19 | 19 | 12 |

1 Create a line plot of the data.

2 How many students are in the class? _____

3 What is the fastest typing speed in the class? _____

4 What is the slowest typing speed in the class? _____

5 What is the range of the data? _____

6 How many students can type 12 words per minute? _____

BRAIN STRETCH

Rafat has a collection of 781 trading cards.
Jose has 60 more trading cards than Rafat.
Edward has twice as many as Jose.
How many trading cards does Edward have?

1 A teacher asks 84 students to get into groups of 4. Let *g* represent the number of groups. Write an equation to help you find *g*.

_____ ☐ _____ = _____

g = _____

2 Compare the expressions using <, >, or =.

$(16 \div 4) + 10$ ☐ $6 + 7$

3 Extend the pattern.

555, 565, 575, 585, _____, _____

What is the rule? _____

_____

4 Write an equation to describe the output rule. Complete the table.

Rule: _____

Input	*x*	20	40	80	100	120
Output	*y*	10	20	40		

1 Write 678,531 in words.

_____

_____

_____

2 Order the numbers from least to greatest.

2,878,495   2,778,415   2,879,415

_____ < _____ < _____

3 Which product is **not** equivalent to 10 × 30?

A. 10 × 3   B. 1 × 300   C. 3 × 100

4 Divide. Use words, pictures, or equations to show your work.

$355 \div 4 =$

WEDNESDAY — Fractions

1 Write the fraction as a decimal.

$$\frac{24}{100}$$

2 Compare the decimals using <, >, or =.

0.66 ☐ 0.66

3 A muffin recipe calls for $\frac{2}{4}$ cup of milk, $\frac{1}{4}$ cup of oil, and $\frac{3}{4}$ cup of orange juice. How much liquid is needed to make the muffins? Draw a model to show your work.

4 Multiply. Simplify your answer if you can.

$$2 \times \frac{3}{4} =$$

THURSDAY — Geometry

1 Draw and label ray *WX*. Draw a point *T* on it.

2 Classify the angles in this triangle.

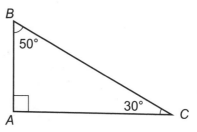

∠ABC _____

∠BAC _____

∠ACB _____

3 How many right angles does this parallelogram have? _____

Which line segments on the parallelogram are parallel?

_____

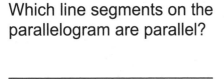

Measurement and Data

Complete the line graph using the information from the data table.

Plant Growth

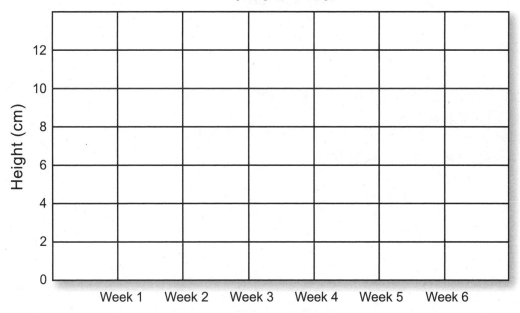

End of Week	Height (cm)
Week 1	2
Week 2	4
Week 3	6
Week 4	8
Week 5	10
Week 6	12

1 At the end of which week(s) was the plant taller than 10 cm? _____

2 How much did the plant grow from the end of week 1 to the end of week 2? _____

3 At the end of which week(s) was the plant no more than 4 cm? _____

4 What was the range of the height of the plant? _____

5 What was the height of the plant at the end of week 5? _____

6 What do you notice about the increase in height from week to week?

_____

BRAIN STRETCH

How are the attributes of a square and a rhombus the same?

MONDAY — Operations and Algebraic Thinking

1 Compare the expressions using <, >, or =.

$(7 + 2) \times 7$ ☐ $80 - 10$

2 Circle the multiples of 8.

60   56   80   72

3 You need 20 light bulbs, but the light bulbs are sold in packages of 3.
How many packages should you buy?
How many extra light bulbs will you get?

4 Write the first 5 terms of this pattern:

Start at 700 and subtract 25 each time.

_____, _____, _____, _____, _____

TUESDAY — Operations in Base Ten

1 Round the number to the nearest ten.

208,323 _____

2 Make the least possible number with these digits (no decimals).

4 2 9 6 7 1 _____

3 $7,193.70
      − $5,946.79

4 Multiply. Use words, pictures, or equations to show your work.

115 × 80 =

WEDNESDAY · Fractions

1 Put the fractions in order from least to greatest. Draw a model to show your work.

$$\frac{2}{9} \qquad \frac{2}{4} \qquad \frac{2}{8} \qquad \frac{2}{3}$$

2 Write the amount in decimal form.

three-tenths

3 Add. Simplify your answer.

$$\frac{2}{6} + \frac{2}{6}$$

4 On Jill's farm, the animals have 6 acres of farmland to graze. Cows graze on $\frac{1}{3}$ of the farmland. On how many acres of land do the cows graze?

THURSDAY · Geometry

1 Name a quadrilateral that has:
- four sides of equal length
- opposite sides parallel
- no right angles

_____

2 Classify the angles in this triangle.

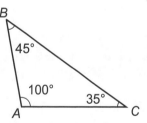

∠ABC _____

∠BAC _____

∠ACB _____

3 Find the unknown angle measure.

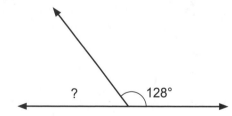

1 Draw a line $1\frac{1}{2}$ inches long.

2 1 year = _____ minutes

7 years = _____ days

10 years = _____ months

3 What are the perimeter and area of a room 8 ft. wide and 9 ft. long? Will a square rug with an area of 49 ft.^{2} fit in the room? Justify your answer.

Perimeter = _____

Area = _____

4 At the store, you spend $1.50 on candy and $1.50 on chips. You give your sister and your brother $1.50 each to buy a drink. How much money did you spend at the store in total? If you had $10 when you went to the store, how much money do you have left?

5 When a clock's hands are exactly on 12 and 1, the angle formed measures 30°. What is the measure of the angle formed when a clock's hands are

a) on the 12 and the 6?
b) on the 12 and the 3?

BRAIN STRETCH

Lucy invited 9 friends over for a party. She has 3.5 L of juice to pour into glasses. If each glass holds 250 mL of juice, does she have enough juice for her and her friends to each have 2 glasses? Justify your answer.

1 Write the related multiplication and division sentences to complete the fact family.

$3 \times 12 = 36$

2 Mrs. Mills bought a box of cereal for $3.36. She also bought milk. She spent a total of $5.86. Let m represent the cost of the milk. Write an equation to help you find m.

_____ ☐ _____ = _____

$m =$ _____

3 There are 134 students going camping. If each bus holds 30 students, how many buses are needed?

4 Extend the pattern.

1, 2, 2, 3, 3, 3, 4, 4, 4, 4, _____, _____, _____
What is the rule?

TUESDAY   Operations in Base Ten

1 Write the number in standard form.

$500,000 + 70,000 + 3,000 + 900$

= _____

2 Order the numbers from greatest to least.

152,080   180,520   150,280

_____ > _____ > _____

3 What number is 1,000 less than 50,800?

4 Divide. Use words, pictures, or equations to show your work.

$600 \div 106 =$

WEDNESDAY — Fractions

1 Compare the decimals using <, >, or =.

0.75 ☐ 0.11

2 Color the circles to show $\frac{5}{7}$ of 14.

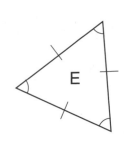

3 Subtract. Simplify your answer.

$9\frac{6}{7} - 1\frac{5}{7} =$

4 Lisa says $\frac{1}{7} + \frac{2}{7} + \frac{5}{7}$ is equal to $1\frac{1}{7}$. Is she correct? Justify your answer.

THURSDAY — Geometry

Which triangles match each description?

equilateral _____

scalene _____

isosceles _____

acute _____

obtuse _____

right _____

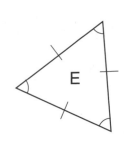
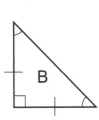
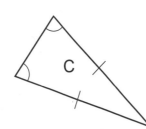
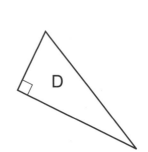

This is a line plot of the shoes sold at the Shoe Shop between Monday and Thursday:

Sizes of Shoes Sold

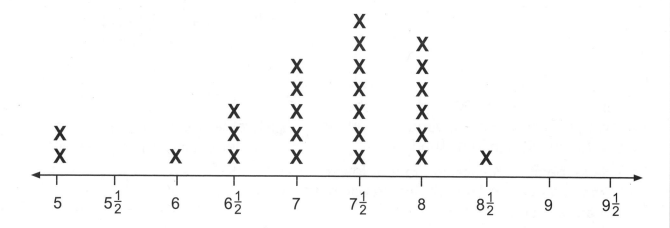

1 On Friday, the Shoe Shop sells five more pairs of shoes in these sizes:

$5\frac{1}{2}$, 6, 6, 8, $8\frac{1}{2}$

Add this data to the line plot.

2 What were the most popular shoe sizes at the store this week? _____

3 What is the difference in size between the largest shoes sold and the smallest shoes sold this week? _____

4 How many people bought size 6 shoes this week? _____

BRAIN STRETCH

How many squares can you find?

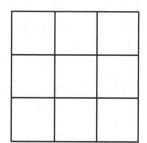

MONDAY — Operations and Algebraic Thinking

1 Fill in the blank to make the equation true.

____ × 6 = 25 + 5

2 a) Is 48 a multiple of 2? How do you know?

b) Is 50 a multiple of 5? How do you know?

3 Fadi spilled a box of 100 marbles in the hallway at school. Karen found 21 marbles, Suda found 21, and Tim found 17.

a) Have the students found more or fewer than half of the marbles? Use an estimate to answer this question.

b) How many marbles are still missing?

4 Create a repeating geometric pattern using any shapes you choose.

TUESDAY — Operations in Base Ten

1 Round the number to the nearest million.

2,455,788

_____

2 Write 781,335 in words.

_____

_____

_____

3 Complete the pattern.

49 ÷ 7 = 7

490 ÷ 7 = _____

4,900 ÷ 7 = _____

4 Multiply. Use words, pictures, or equations to show your work.

4,297 × 4 =

1 Write the decimal as a fraction.

0.57

2 Subtract. Simplify your answer.

$7\dfrac{4}{5} - 5\dfrac{3}{5} =$

3 Write $2\dfrac{1}{3}$ as a sum of fractions.

4 There are 50 students in the schoolyard. If $\dfrac{2}{5}$ are girls, how many boys are there? Draw a model to show your work.

THURSDAY Geometry

1 Which shape does **not** have four right angles?

A. square B. rectangle C. parallelogram

2 Draw an obtuse triangle. Measure and label the angles.

3 Draw a line of symmetry.

4 Write an equation to help you find $\angle PQO$ and $\angle MQN$.

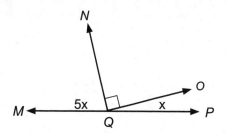

This is the new wall in front of the library in Sprucetown:

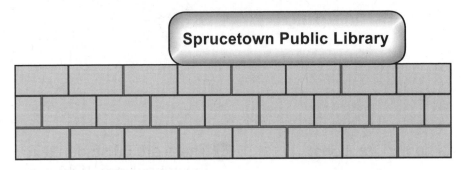

1 The wall is 12 feet long and 3 feet high. Find the measurements in inches.

12 ft. = _____ in.   3 ft. = _____ in.

2 Find the length and height of each rectangular block in the wall. Give your answer in feet and inches.

length of block = _____ ft. = _____ in.

height of block = _____ ft. = _____ in.

3 Circle the two blocks in the wall that look different from the others.

What is their length and width? _____

4 The firefighters wants to build a wall with the same height and width in front of the fire station but they have square blocks with sides that measure 1 foot. Design a wall for the firefighters. How many blocks are in your wall?

_____

BRAIN STRETCH

Which 3D shape will this net make?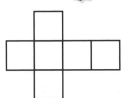

Fraction Strips

		1

$\frac{1}{2}$	$\frac{1}{2}$

$\frac{1}{3}$	$\frac{1}{3}$	$\frac{1}{3}$

$\frac{1}{4}$	$\frac{1}{4}$	$\frac{1}{4}$	$\frac{1}{4}$

$\frac{1}{5}$	$\frac{1}{5}$	$\frac{1}{5}$	$\frac{1}{5}$	$\frac{1}{5}$

$\frac{1}{6}$	$\frac{1}{6}$	$\frac{1}{6}$	$\frac{1}{6}$	$\frac{1}{6}$	$\frac{1}{6}$

$\frac{1}{7}$	$\frac{1}{7}$	$\frac{1}{7}$	$\frac{1}{7}$	$\frac{1}{7}$	$\frac{1}{7}$	$\frac{1}{7}$

$\frac{1}{8}$	$\frac{1}{8}$	$\frac{1}{8}$	$\frac{1}{8}$	$\frac{1}{8}$	$\frac{1}{8}$	$\frac{1}{8}$	$\frac{1}{8}$

$\frac{1}{9}$	$\frac{1}{9}$	$\frac{1}{9}$	$\frac{1}{9}$	$\frac{1}{9}$	$\frac{1}{9}$	$\frac{1}{9}$	$\frac{1}{9}$	$\frac{1}{9}$

$\frac{1}{10}$	$\frac{1}{10}$	$\frac{1}{10}$	$\frac{1}{10}$	$\frac{1}{10}$	$\frac{1}{10}$	$\frac{1}{10}$	$\frac{1}{10}$	$\frac{1}{10}$	$\frac{1}{10}$

0.1	0.1	0.1	0.1	0.1	0.1	0.1	0.1	0.1	0.1

$\frac{1}{11}$	$\frac{1}{11}$	$\frac{1}{11}$	$\frac{1}{11}$	$\frac{1}{11}$	$\frac{1}{11}$	$\frac{1}{11}$	$\frac{1}{11}$	$\frac{1}{11}$	$\frac{1}{11}$	$\frac{1}{11}$

$\frac{1}{12}$	$\frac{1}{12}$	$\frac{1}{12}$	$\frac{1}{12}$	$\frac{1}{12}$	$\frac{1}{12}$	$\frac{1}{12}$	$\frac{1}{12}$	$\frac{1}{12}$	$\frac{1}{12}$	$\frac{1}{12}$	$\frac{1}{12}$

Math — Show What You Know!

_____

☐ I read the question and I know what I need to find.

☐ I drew a picture or a diagram to help solve the question.

☐ I showed all the steps in solving the question.

☐ I used math language to explain my thinking.

Core Learning Standards for Mathematics Grade 4

Student																					93

Level 1 Student demonstrates limited comprehension of the math concept when applying math skills.

Level 2 Student demonstrates adequate comprehension of the math concept when applying math skills.

Level 3 Student demonstrates proficient comprehension of the math concept when applying math skills.

Level 4 Student demonstrates thorough comprehension of the math concept when applying math skills.

Week 1, pages 1–3

Monday   **1.** B   **2.** (X)   **3.** A. P   B. C   C. P   **4.** 111

Tuesday   **1.** 5   **2.** 137,880   **3.** >   **4.** 70

Wednesday   **1.** 2/5   **2.** <   **3.** 2/10   **4.** 1/8, 2/8

Thursday   **1.** Sample answer: •B   **2.** B   **3.** 1   **4.** A

Friday   **1.** 24, 36, 48   **2.** 1,400 m   **3.** Any 9 adjacent squares should be shaded, various perimeters can occur.

     4. 1:45

Brain Stretch   **a)** $130.00   **b)** 11:30 a.m.   **c)** $4.75

Week 2, pages 4–6

Monday   **1.** A   **2.** 41   **3.** $c < 22$ **4.** 10, 16, 22, 28, 34

Tuesday   **1.** 500 ones   **2.** 200,000   **3.** 3,900   **4.** 49

Wednesday   **1.** 3/12   **2.** >   **3.** 0.11   **4.** 6

Thursday   **1.** Sample answer: B ——→ A   **2.** A (and C)

     3. Pentagon; 5 obtuse angles; 0 acute angles   **4.** B

Friday   **1.** 205   **2.** Michael   **3.** Spencer and Megan   **4.** 65   **5.** 15   **6.** 5   **7.** 20

Brain Stretch   Vivienne is the oldest. Tina is the youngest.

Week 3, pages 7–9

Monday   **1.** 4 × 4   **2.** 11 is prime because there are only 2 rectangles: 1 × 11 and 11 × 1.   **2.**   **3.** y = Kas's age – 10

     4. Sample answer: ○○○●●○○○○

Tuesday   **1.** 400 tens   **2.** 300   **3.** <   **4.** 3,600

Wednesday   **1.** 1/3   **2.** 1/2, 2/4. 6/12   **3.** 1 + 1/4   **4.**

Thursday   **1.** Sample answer: A ←——→ B   **2.** Square   **3.** A   **4.** B

Friday   **1.** 200 cm, 300 cm, 400 cm   **2.** 1,000 years   **3.** Yes, because Abdullah has a total of 3 pints of milk, and

     4 pints could fit in the gallon jug.   **4. a)** Add the length of all 8 sides. **b)** 72 ft

Brain Stretch   **a)** 400 square yards   **b)** 300 feet   **c)** $1,000

Week 4, pages 10–12

Monday   **1.** A   **2.** 3 + 2   **3.** A. C   B. C   C. C   **4.** 160, 320, 640 Double the previous number.

Tuesday   **1.** 60 ones   **2.** 46,227   **3.** 80,833   **4.** 4, with no remainder.

Wednesday   **1.** Look for a model showing 0.4 < 0.5.   **2.** 40/100   **3.** >   **4.** 0.42

Thursday   **1.** Sample answer: A ●——● B   **2.** Hexagon; 6 obtuse angles; 0 acute angles   **3.** D   **4.** B

Friday   **1.** 24, 36   **2.** 1 hr. 3 min.   **3.** $9   **4.** Answers will vary.

Brain Stretch   Both designs do not have the same area. Different shapes with the same perimeter

will not have the same area.

Week 5, pages 13–15

Monday **1.** 5 × 8 **2.** 800, 820, 840, 860, 880

3. Sample answer: **a)** 440; I rounded 164 to 200, 39 to 40, and 193 to 200. **b)** 396 **4.** 3, 9

Tuesday **1.** > **2.** 4,000 **3.** 976,431 **4.** 8,256

Wednesday **1.** Do not agree. Picture should show 21 shaded squares in one hundred grid and 60 shaded squares

in the other. **2. a)** same **b)** 1, 2; 3, 6; 1, 2 **3.** 0.9 **4.** 7/8

Thursday **1.** Sample answer: G •——— P • ———• H **2.** Sample answer:

3. Two **4.** Octagon; 8 obtuse angles; 0 acute angles

Friday Shading should extend to 17 for Blue, 7 for Silver, 13 for Red, and 6 for Black. **1.** 1 **2.** 6 **3.** 43

Brain Stretch **a)** 1,520 **b)** 380 brown and 1,140 white

Week 6, pages 16–18

Monday **1.** $x = 5$ **2.** $85 + c$ **3.** 150 **4.** A

Tuesday **1.** 90 tens **2.** 10,300 < 10,322 < 10,364 **3.** 10 × 3 = 30; 2 × 20 = 40; 2 × 3 = 6; 30 + 40 + 6 = 276

4. $85.08

Wednesday **1. a)** 12; 3 **b)** The total number of squares is different. 1/3 is different in each grid. **2.** > **3.** 0.07

4. a) Look for a model showing 2 × 1 1/2 **b)** 4 1/2 miles

Thursday **1.** **2.** acute **3.** B **4.** C

Friday **1.** 6, 9, 12 **2.** 2,496,000 meters **3.** 4 1/2 h; 120, 180, 240, 300 **4.** Perimeter = 18 units; Area = 14

square units

Brain Stretch **1.** Mrs. Kumar should buy 16 boxes of cupcakes. 16 × 6 = 96 cupcakes for 23 × 4 = 92 students.

There will be 4 extra cupcakes, enough for the teachers

Week 7, pages 19–21

Monday **1.** 2 × 10 **2.** 2, 6, 18, 54, 162 **3.** A. C B. C C. P **4.** 25 cups of milk

Tuesday **1.** 600,000 **2.** 129,500 **3.** 98 **4.** 9,554

Wednesday **1.** Sample answer: Look for an area model showing 1/4 = 2/8.

2. 5/10 = 1/10 + **1**/10 + 3/10; 5/10 = 2/10 + **3**/10 **3.** =

4. Disagree. 55 of the squares should be shaded in one grid and 20 in the other.

Thursday **1.** **2.** M •——— X • ———• N **3.** A **4.** Rectangle

Friday **1.** 12,000 mL **2.** 40 years **3.** $7.14 **4.** Perimeter = 38 yd.; Area = 84 sq. yd.

Brain Stretch **a)** 15 **b)** $45 **c)** 45 games

Week 8, pages 22–24

Monday   **1.** $b = 5$ **2.** C   **3.** 32, 64; Double the previous number.   **4.**

Tuesday   **1.** 300 ones   **2.** >   **3.** Seventeen thousand, four hundred

              4. 3 R2 ●●●●●●●●|●●●●●●●●|●●●●●●●●|●●

Wednesday   **1.** 4/9   **2.** **50**/100   **3.** >   **4.** 5/7

Thursday   **1.** Sample answer: **2.** obtuse   **3.** 45°   **4.** A

Friday   **1.** 20 cups   **2.** 24 hr.   **3.** Yes. The number line should show arrival at 10:00.

              4. Perimeter = 24 units; Area = 15 square units

Brain Stretch   Sample answer: counting time, counting money, figuring out a grade, calculating distance, dividing snacks

Week 9, pages 25–27

Monday   **1.** 8 × 5 = 40, 40 ÷ 8 = 5, 40 ÷ 5 = 8   **2.** 8   **3.** 7   **4. a)** 500 **b)** Sample answer: The numbers alternate

              between ending in 0 or 5. They are all multiples of 5.

Tuesday   **1.** 100,000   **2.** Three hundred seventy-eight thousand, six hundred seventy-four   **3.** 20,000

              4. 3 R1 ●●●●●|●●●●●|●●●●●|●

Wednesday   **1.** Look for an area model showing that 5/8 is greater than 1/2.   **2.** >   **3.** 0.99

              4. Sample answer: 4/6 = 3/6 + 1/6

Thursday   **1.** Sample answer: D   E   **2.**   acute   **3.** 137°   **4.** A or C

Friday   **1.** 6   **2.** 40   **3.** John   **4.** 24   **5.** 32

Brain Stretch   **a)** A dozen for $5.99 is the better buy since $0.60 × 12 = $7.20   **b)** $4.01

Week 10, pages 28–30

Monday   **1.** 7   **2.** A. C B. C C. P   **3.** 2 × 10 = 20

              4. Sample answer: Begin at 10 and add 5 five each time: 10, 15, 20, 25, 30

Tuesday   **1.** 7,000   **2.** 982,400   **3.** One hundred seventy-eight thousand, nine hundred

              4. 100; There are 100 fours in 400.

Wednesday   **1.** **70**/100   **2.** 1/5, 3/5, 4/5   **3.** >   **4.** 1/2; 3/2

Thursday   **1.** Sample answer: **2.** acute

              3. Right triangle; 0 obtuse angles; 2 acute angles

              4. The first and third figures should be circled.

Friday   **1.** 20,000 cm   **2.** 365 days   **3.** Sample answer: 2 quarters, 1 nickel, 3 pennies; or 5 dimes, 1 nickel and

              3 pennies. The fewest number of coins is 6.   **4.** 46 ft².

Brain Stretch   **a)** 99 m   **b)** 432 people   **c)** 4 p.m.

Week 11, pages 31–33

Monday **1.** 3 slices each   **2.** $y = 5x$; 40, 50 **3.** 3, 5, 7, 11, 13 **4.** <

Tuesday **1.** 9,000 hundreds **2.** 670,000 **3.** 5 ⣿ ⣿ ⣿ ⣿ ⣿ **4.** 3,314

Wednesday **1.** 4/7 **2.** **60**/100 **3.** > **4.** **60**/100

Thursday **1.** ∠ acute **2.** Triangle; 0 obtuse angles; 3 acute angles **3.** 0 **4.** D

Friday **1.** 900 seconds, 360 minutes, 30 minutes **2.** $2.50 **3.** 24 ft. **4.** Perimeter = 28 m; Area = 49 m²

Brain Stretch **a)** Claire would have to plant 176 tulips next year to reach her goal of 300. **b)** Yes

   c) sample amswer: 6 × 9 = 54 last year, plus 70 this year is 124. 300 − 124 = 176

Week 12, pages 34–36

Monday **1.** 7 × 3 **2.** 20 **3.** Estimate of $60 left over. Round 18 up to 20, round 11 down to 10. 90 − 20 − 10 = 60

4. Sample answer: ○●●○●●

Tuesday **1.** < **2.** 973 **3.** 4,214 **4.** 1,372,013

Wednesday **1. a)** 5/10 **b)** Multiply the numerator and the denominator by the same number.

   2. Sample answer: Look for an area model showing 6/9 = 2/3. **3.** 1/7, 3/7, 5/7 **4.** 0.2

Thursday **1.** A●——D●——●B **2.** A **3.** ∠ obtuse **4.** The first two figures should be circled.

Friday **1.** January **2.** May **3.** 25 **4.** 20 **5.** 55

Brain Stretch 17 jelly beans

Week 13, pages 37–39

Monday **1.** 8 × 6 **2.** 1, 30; 2, 15; 3, 10; 5, 6 **3.** 8 × 7 = y **4.** 55, 66; Start at 11 and add 11 each time.

Tuesday **1.** 60 ten thousands **2.** 528,730 **3.** 3 R2 ●●●● | ●●●● | ●●●● | ●● **4.** 10,344

Wednesday **1.** 12/**14** **2.** 3/4 **3.** **98**/100 **4.** Sample answer: 6/6 + 6/6 + 6/6 + 1/6

Thursday **1.** ∠ acute **2.** 135° **3.** Answers include: square, rectangle, parallelogram, rhombus **4.** similar

Friday **1.** Lines should measure 25 mm. **2.** 7 hr. **3.** 8:30 a.m. **4.** 30 ft.

Brain Stretch Rounding estimate is $4 change. Exact change is $5.60.

Week 14, pages 40–42

Monday **1.** 49, 63, 70 **2.** 36 **3.** $7, $21 **4.** $y = 5x$; 20, 25

Tuesday **1.** $141.36 **2.** 1,000,000 **3.** 473 × 4 = (**400** × 4) + (**70** × 4) + (**3** × 4) = 1,892

Wednesday **1.** Sample answer: 6/14 **2.** 3/4, 1/2, 1/4 **3.** 6/10 **4.** 10/3 ▦▦ ▦▦ ▦▦ ▦▦ ▦▢

Thursday **1.** obtuse **2.** ∠ acute **3.** 2 pairs of parallel sides **4.** B (or A)

Friday **1.** Kate **2.** Julia, James, Eric **3.** 40 **4.** 25 **5.** 80 **6.** Olivia

Brain Stretch The volume of 4 jugs is more than 2 pints. 4 cups = 2 pints = j; therefore $4j$ > 2 pints.

Week 15, pages 43–45

Monday **1.** 4 × 7 = 28, 28 ÷ 4 = 7, 28 ÷ 7 = 4 **2.** 8 **3.** 4, 40, 400, 4,000 , 40,000 **4.** 25 min. 75 ÷ 3 = 25

Tuesday **1.** 790,000 **2.** 77,911 < 77,918 < 88,791 **3.** 75 **4.** 285

Wednesday **1.** 16/**20** **2.** 1/4 **3.** 7/10 **4.** 1

Thursday **1.** **2.** 4 **3.** **4.** D

Friday Shading should extend to 54 for Class A, 42 for B, 48 for C, 36 for D, and 60 for E **1.** Class E **2.** 24

3. Class D **4.** Class E, Class A, Class C, Class B, Class D **5.** 2

Brain Stretch 13 jars and 4 cartons

Week 16, pages 46–48

Monday **1.** 4j **2.** y = x − 5; 19, 25 **3.** 810; 8,100; 81,000 **4.** =

Tuesday **1.** 200 tens **2.** twenty-four thousand, six hundred seventy-one **3.** 3,890

4. 112 − 70 = 42; 42 − 42 = 0; 10 + 6 = 16

Wednesday **1.** 1/3 **2.** 1/2 **3.** 3 1/3 **4.** 6

Thursday **1.** obtuse **2.** 360° **3.** Parallelogram, 2 obtuse angles, 2 acute angles **4.** congruent

Friday **1.** **2.** 3/4 hr. **3.** 390 min.

Brain Stretch Sample answer: 1 and 3 1/4, 1 1/4 and 3 1/2, 1 1/2 and 3 3/4

Week 17, pages 49–51

Monday **1.** 1, 72; 2, 36; 3, 24; 4, 18; 6, 12; 7, 8 **2.** 8 days, 32 ÷ 4 = 8

3. Sample answer: Begin at 100 and subtract 5 each time. 100, 95, 90, 85, 80 **4.** >

Tuesday **1.** 500 ones **2.** 451,760 **3.** 60, 600 **4.** 80

Wednesday **1.** 30/100 **2.** 7/8 **3.** 5/10 **4.** 6/5

Thursday **1.** Sample answer: **2.** An angle that measures 180°. **3.** trapezoid **4.** 108°

Friday **1.** 1,120 oz. **2.** C **3.** 112 min. **4.** 36 yd.

Brain Stretch 49 papers

Week 18, pages 52–54

Monday **1.** 9 × 6 = 54, 54 ÷ 9 = 6, 54 ÷ 6 = 9 **2.** 8 times as much **3.** 2.5 **4.** 40

Tuesday **1.** 2,225,680 **2.** 17,432 > 17,324 > 14,723 **3.** 117 × 2 = (**100** × 2) + (**10** × 2) + (**7** × 2) = **234**

Wednesday **1.** Sample answer: 5/6 **2.** 3/8 **3.** 2 **4.** 1 1/2 cups

Thursday   **1.** ∠ acute   **2.** A, B, E   **3.** 0   **4.** 5

Friday   **1.** 10 cm   **2.** April   **3.** 14 cm   **4.** 14 cm   **5.** 18 cm

Brain Stretch   Sample answer: 1 1/4 and 4 3/4, 1 1/2 and 4 1/2, 1 3/4 and 4 1/4

Week 19, pages 55–57

Monday   **1.** 6 × 5   **2.** 12 classrooms, 36 ÷ 3 = 12   **3.** ▓   **4.** Sample answer: LOOKLOOK

Tuesday   **1.** 4 tens   **2.** <   **3.** 80,828   **4.** 12 R2; Sample equation: 12 + 12 + 12 + 12 + 2 = 50

Wednesday   **1.** 5/21   **2.** Sample answer: 3/6 + 1/6   **3.** 4 3/5   **4.** <

Thursday   **1.** Sample answer: [diagram with points J, K, B, C]   **2.** [right angle diagram] right angle   **3.** 68°   **4.** A

Friday   **1.** 2,555 days; 120 months   **2.** 1,000   **3.** $2   **4.** Perimeter = 137 ft.; Area = 242.5 sq. ft.

Brain Stretch   7 tins; 6 full tins, plus a 7ᵗʰ for the last 34 marbles.

Week 20, pages 58–60

Monday   **1.** 19 × 2 = 38, 38 ÷ 19 = 2, 38 ÷ 2 = 19   **2.** 4 times more.   **3.** (56)   **4.** 300; 3,000; 30,000

Tuesday   **1.** 110   **2.** 690,000   **3.** 107,620

4. 8

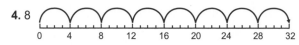

```
0   4   8   12   16   20   24   28   32
```

Wednesday   **1.** 1/2   **2.** 95/100   **3.** 0.45   **4.** 2 1/4 cups

Thursday   **1.** [angle diagram] obtuse   **2.** 103°   **3.** C   **4.** 0, AD and BC

Friday   **1.** 4 pints   **2.** 10   **3.** 3.9 min (or 3 min and 54 sec)   **4.** 38 yd.

Brain Stretch   **a)** Need at least 12 classes. **b)** Yes **c)** sample answer: 67 + 29 = 96; 96 ÷ 8 = 12

Week 21, pages 61–63

Monday   **1.** <   **2.** 1, 24; 2, 12; 3, 8; 4, 6   **3.** 6 × y = 24, 24 ÷ 6 = y   **4.** 20, 0; Start at 100 and subtract 20 each time.

Tuesday   **1.** 90,000 ones   **2.** 5   **3.** 144; Sample model: 16 + 16 + 16 + 16 + 16 + 16 + 16 + 16 + 16   **4.** $666.91

Wednesday   **1.** Sample answer: 13/9   **2.** =   **3.** [fraction bar models] 2 2/7

4. 4 2/3 hours (or 4 hr. and 40 min.)

Thursday   **1.** [diagram with points U, V, D, E]   **2.** [angle diagram] obtuse   **3.** kite   **4.** A

Friday   **1.** 12   **2.** [line plot]

```
                    x    x
                    x    x
      x    x    x   x    x    x    x    x
    13  13 1/4 13 1/2 13 3/4  14  14 1/4 14 1/2 14 3/4
```

   3. 1 3/4 inches

Brain Stretch   **a)** 5.3 km   **b)** 0.7 km

Week 22, pages 64–66

Monday   **1.** 12 × 11 = *p*, *p* = 132   **2.** ㉛   **3.** <   **4.** S

Tuesday   **1.** 75,964   **2.** 153,087

           3. Sample answer: There are 2 ones in 532 and 2 tens in 523. 20 is 10 times greater than 2.   **4.** 11

Wednesday   **1.** 25/7   **2.** 10 1/2   **3.** <   **4.** 1/2 tablespoon

Thursday   **1.** F•——•G / P•——•Q   **2.** acute   **3.** 60°   **4.** B

Friday   **1.** 12 cm   **2.** 2 cm   **3.** 14 cm   **4.** 14 cm   **5.** 4 cm

Brain Stretch   Sample answer: A rectangular prism, because it stacks well.

Week 23, pages 67–69

Monday   **1.** 6 ft.   **2.** ⑥⓪ 72 ⑩⓪ ②⓪   **3.** 280; 2,800; 28,000

           4. Sample answer: Rule: Alternate A and B; A, B, A, B, A

Tuesday   **1.** 24   **2.** 400,000   **3.** C   **4.** 110; Sample answer: 22 is made of two 11s. 10 times more than 22 is 220.

           So there must be 110 twos in 220.

Wednesday   **1.** 8/15   **2.** 0.5   **3.** 3 1/2   **4.** 1 5/9

Thursday   **1.** Sample answer: 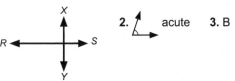   **2.** acute   **3.** B   **4.** similar

Friday   **1.** 4,000 g   **2.** 260   **3.** 12 ft.

           4. Room A with a perimeter = 34 ft. and area = 70 sq. ft. (Room B: Perimeter = 30 ft., area = 54 sq. ft.)

Brain Stretch   1 1/2 lb. of potatoes

Week 24, pages 70–72

Monday   **1.** 2,100   **2.** *y* = × *x* 6; 36, 30   **3.** 1, 77; 7, 11

           4. His friends got 6 bars each. His brother got 2 bars.

Tuesday   **1.** =   **2.** 986,023   **3.** 40, 400   **4.** 121; Eleven 11s is 11 more than ten 11s (which is 110).

Wednesday   **1.** 0.6   **2.** **132**/100   **3.** 4 1/6   **4.** 4 1/2 cups

Thursday   **1.** Triangles should have one 90° angle and the sum of all angles should equal 180°.   **2.** ▱

           3. C   **4.** Sample answer: ⊣■

Friday   **1.** 30 ft., 360 in.   **2.** 8 pt.   **3.** 9:45 p.m.   **4.** Perimeter = 280 cm; Area = 4,000 cm²

Brain Stretch   Yes. Each six-pack of tickets is one ride for all 3 friends. So they can go on 9 rides each.

Week 25, pages 73–75

Monday   **1.** $20   **2.** 42, 44   **3.** 70; Start at 40 and add 6 each time.   **4.** 61, 72, 83, 94, 105

Tuesday   **1.** 824,400   **2.** 10 times   **3.** 6,010; Multiplying by 10 adds a zero.   **4.** 534,295

Wednesday   **1.** 1/3   **2.** 12 2/3   **3.** 0.07   **4.** 22

           © **Chalkboard Publishing**

Thursday   **1.**    **2.** B

         3. 90° = 2x + x, 90° = 3x, x = 30°, therefore ∠POQ = 60° and ∠QOR = 30°   **4.** A

Friday   **1.** 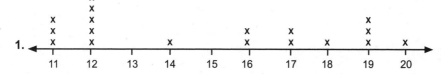   **2.** 2 days   **3.** 1 5/8 pies, 13 slices

Brain Stretch   Sample answer: With a string.

Week 26, pages 76–78

Monday   **1.** Sample answer: about 150 cans; I multiplied 3 × 6 = 18 and 5 × 6 = 30. That's about 50. I need 200 so

        50 + 50 is 100 and then I need another 100.   **2.** <   **3.** 4 candies each

        4. Sample answer: o, oo, oooo, oooooooo

Tuesday   **1.** 546,000   **2.** Three hundred nine thousand, seven hundred sixty-two   **3.** 101,377 < 108,323 < 110,733

        4. 11; Seven goes into 7 once and into 70 ten times.

Wednesday   **1.** 0.8   **2.** 8 8/9   **3.** 3   **4.** 1 2/3 gallons

Thursday   **1.** S •——————H——————• T   **2.** right   **3.** C   **4.** 45°

```
                    x
                    x
       x            x
       x            x                    x            x
       x            x           x        x       x    x        x
    ───┼────────────┼───────────┼────────┼───────┼────┼────────┼───►
       11           12          13   14  15   16  17   18   19  20
```

Friday   **1.** (number line plot above)

        2. 18   **3.** 20 wpm   **4.** 11 wpm   **5.** 9   **6.** 5 students

Brain Stretch   1,682 trading cards

Week 27, pages 79–81

Monday   **1.** 84 ÷ 4 = g, g = 21   **2.** >   **3.** 595, 605; Start at 555 and add 10 each time.   **4.** y = × x 2; 50, 60

Tuesday   **1.** Six hundred seventy-eight thousand, five hundred thirty-one   **2.** 2,778,415 < 2,878,495 < 2,879,415

        3. A   **4.** 88 R3

Wednesday   **1.** 0.24   **2.** =   **3.** 6/4 cups or 1 1/2 cups   **4.** 1 1/2

Thursday   **1.** W •———T———► X   **2.** ∠ABC acute, ∠BAC right, ∠ACB acute   **3.** 0, DG and EF, DE and GF

Friday   On the graph, shading should extend to 2 cm for Week 1, 4 cm for Week 2, 6 cm for Week 3, 8 cm for

        Week 4, 10 cm for Week 5, and 12 cm for Week 6   **1.** Week 6   **2.** 2 cm   **3.** Weeks 1 and 2   **4.** 10 cm

        5. 10 cm   **6.** It grew 2 cm each week.

Brain Stretch   They each have 4 equal sides. They each have 4 angles. Opposite sides are parallel.

        Opposite angles are equal.

Week 28, pages 82–84

Monday   **1.** <   **2.** 60 ⑤⑥ ⑧⓪ ⑦②   **3.** 7 packages, one extra   **4.** 700, 675, 650, 625, 600

Tuesday   **1.** 208,320   **2.** 124,679   **3.** $1,246.91   **4.** 9,200

Wednesday   **1.** 2/9, 2/8, 2/4, 2/3   **2.** 0.3   **3.** 2/3   **4.** 2 acres

Thursday   **1.** Rhombus   **2.** ∠*ABC* is acute, ∠*BAC* is obtuse, ∠*ACB* is acute   **3.** 52°

Friday   **1.** Lines should measure 1.5 inches.   **2.** 525,600 minutes, 2,555 days, 120 months

     3. Perimeter = 34 ft.; Area = 72 sq. ft. A rug will fit in the room since each side is only 7 ft. long.

     4. Spent $6, have $4 left.   **5. a)** 180° **b)** 90°

Brain Stretch   Lucy has 14 glasses of juice, not enough for each person to have 2 glasses.

Week 29, pages 85–87

Monday   **1.** 12 × 3 = 36, 36 ÷ 3 = 12, 36 ÷ 12 = 3   **2.** $5.86 – $3.36 = *m*, *m* = $2.50

     3. 4 R 14; Five buses are needed because the students cannot fit on 4 buses.

     4. 5, 5, 5; Start at 1 and write each numeral the number of times equal to its value, in turn.

Tuesday   **1.** 573,900   **2.** 180,520 < 150,280 < 152,080   **3.** 49,800   **4.** 5 R70

Wednesday   **1.** >   **2.** 10 circles should be colored.   **3.** 8 1/7   **4.** Lisa is correct. 8/7 = 1 1/7

Thursday   **1.** equilateral: E; scalene: A, G; isosceles: B, C, F; acute: C, E; obtuse: A, F, G; right: B, D

Friday   **1.** (number line with x marks at 5 1/2, 6, 6, 8, 8 1/2)   **2.** 7 1/2 and 8   **3.** 3 1/2   **4.** 3

Brain Stretch   14 squares

Week 30, pages 88–90

Monday   **1.** 5   **2.** Sample answers: **a)** Yes. All even numbers are multiples of 2. **b)** Yes. All numbers ending in 0 are multiples of 5.   **3. a)** More than half **b)** 41   **4.** Answer will vary.

Tuesday   **1.** 2,000,000   **2.** Seven hundred eighty-one thousand, three hundred thirty-five

     3. 70, 700   **4.** 17,188

Wednesday   **1.** 57/100   **2.** 2 1/5   **3.** Sample answer: 6/3 + 1/3   **4.** 30 boys

Thursday   **1.** C   **2.** Sample answer: (triangle with vertices A, B, C)   **3.** (airplane)

     4. 180° = 90° + 5*x* + *x*, 90° = 6*x*, *x* = 15, ∠*PQO* = 15°, ∠*MQN* = 75°

Friday   **1.** 144 in., 36 in.   **2.** Length: 1 1/2 ft. = 18 in.; height: 1 ft. = 12 in.

     3. Length: 9 in., height: 12 in.   **4.** 36 blocks

Brain Stretch   cube